"BEFORE YOU CONSIDER WHAT YOU WILL EAT AND DRINK, CONSIDER
WHOM YOU INTEND TO EAT AND DRINK WITH." - EPICURIUS

Recipes are for four people unless otherwise noted.

Measurements of flour, rice, etc in the original Finnish edition were offered in millilitres rathers than grams.

Bonnier Books have chosen to follow this course in the English edition rather than translate these measurements to grams.

There are a selection of measuring glasses and jugs available for purchase in the UK that are calibrated for measuring solids in millilitres

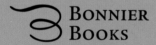

BONNIER BOOKS

Bonnier Books, Appledram Barns, Birdham Road,
Chichester PO20 7EQ
www.bonnierbooks.co.uk
First published in the UK
in 2008 by Bonnier Books
ISBN: 978-1-905825-56-1

Originally published by
Kustannusosakeyhtio Tammi, Helsinki
in 2006 as Hot-chiliä ja muita mauste-elämyksiä

All text stories by Marianne Kiskola
unless otherwise credited.

© Marianne Kiskola and Sanna Miettunen 2006
Photographs by Pia Inberg
Graphic design by Camilla Pentti
Printed in China

Marianne Kiskola
Sanna Miettunen

HOT!
HOT!
HOT!

chilli peppers and other spice experiences

Photographs by Pia Inberg
Translated by Owen Witesman

BONNIER BOOKS

To the Reader

Have you ever burned your fingers with a chilli or happened upon a spice you weren't familiar with in the grocery store? No problem. Hop aboard our spice barge to experience the prized delicacies of the Silk Road and Roman soldiers. Those old familiar friends from your spice shelf, salt and pepper, will be joined not only by chillies, but also by cayenne pepper, cumin, coriander seeds and the vanilla pod. And what on earth is galangal root?

Let us embark together on a journey of taste from Cleopatra's aubergine caviar to chilli cocoa and savour culinary delights in the fascinating company of caraway potatoes and chilli *grissini*.

Enchanting delicacies, enticing illustrations and absurd anecdotes offer a sensory explosion – as herbs and spices are wont to do. We also offer tips on the freezing of herbs, the correct handling of chillies (only masochists put chilli in their eyes!) and other vexing spice mysteries. The majority of the recipes in this book are also designed to be appropriate for those with milk allergies, lactose intolerance and coeliac disease, as well as vegans.

As a voyager on this spice ship, you will need an adventurous and enthusiastic attitude in addition to your saucepan and ladle.

Please join us as we enter the mysterious realm of spices!

Helsinki
6 December 2005

Marianne Kiskola and Sanna Miettunen

TABLE OF CONTENTS

Herbs and Spices

EVIDENCE OF THE USE OF SPICES IN FOOD PREPARATION HAS BEEN FOUND FROM AS FAR BACK AS 6000 YEARS AGO. THE ANCIENT EGYPTIANS USED SPICES IN COSMETICS AND EMBALMING, AS WELL AS FOOD PREPARATION. INDICATIONS OF SPICES BEING USED AS TRADING COMMODITIES ALONGSIDE JEWELS AND GOLD CAN BE FOUND IN THE BIBLE AND TALES FROM THE SILK ROAD. ALTHOUGH SPICES ARE AVAILABLE TO EVERYONE IN OUR DAY, THEY HAVE NOT LOST A BIT OF THEIR VALUE.

BASIL

Basil is one of the world's oldest and most popular spices. In India, large bushes of basil growing around Hindu temples is a common sight. They are considered holy and not meant to be eaten. Thus, the culinary tourist should keep his hands to himself. The ancient Greeks used basil to treat flu, and believed that when mixed with a drop of wine it was good for the eyes.

Basil grows wild in Asia and the lands of the Mediterranean. Consumers farther north are more accustomed to fresh basil at the grocer's coming from the hothouse. Basil may also be grown at home on the windowsill. It needs plenty of water, light and warmth.

Numerous varieties of basil are available in addition to the common strain, including, for example, Thai basil and cinnamon basil.

Basil's flavour and scent is very intense and pleasant.

Basil is also sold dried in jars.

BAY LEAF

The rich, dark green, leathery bay leaf derives from the Mediterranean Bay Laurel tree.

Bay leaves are aromatic and slightly bitter.

Bay promotes erudition, wisdom and honour. In many countries, laurel wreaths are still bestowed upon recipients of the master's degree.

Bay leaves may be found dried on the spice shelf. Check to make sure that the leaves have retained their colour and have not begun to darken or bleach yellow.

CARAWAY

Caraway should not be confused with cumin, which is sometimes known as Roman caraway.

Caraway belongs to the carrot family, along with parsley. Its seeds are often used to season breads and cheeses. The seasoning of bread with caraway is a legacy of Roman soldiers, for whom is was a great delicacy. Later it supplanted the use of cumin in the rest of Europe as well.

CARDAMOM

Cardamom belongs to the same family of spice lilies as ginger and turmeric. It can be found in stores as a powder, crushed, as seeds or as whole seed pods. The seeds are dark and the seed pod is a beautiful green.

Cardamom seeds emit a pleasant smelling oil, which gives the home a delightful fragrance.

Cardamom arrived in the North with the Vikings and has been a long-time staple of Nordic baking.

CAYENNE PEPPER

Cayenne pepper is the fruit of a plant of the *Capsicum* genus, like chillies and the common red/green peppers. Its appearance is similar to that of a long chilli pepper.

It is most commonly found in powdered form.

This spice if quite hot, because the entire fruit, including the seeds, is used in the powder.

CHILLI PEPPERS

Chilli peppers belong to the same *Capsicum* genus as other peppers. Chillies are said to have originated in South America, but nowadays they are used and cultivated widely around the world. The chilli pepper is especially common in Asian, South American, Indian and Caribbean cuisine.

There are hundreds of varieties of chilli pepper, from mild to blazing hot, in different colours, shapes and sizes.

The heat of a chilli pepper is generally indicated in Scoville units, which are based on a taste test developed in the early twentieth century.

For example, the heat of Cayenne pepper is 30,000-50,000 and Habanero is 570,000.

Many chilli products use simpler ratings such as a 1-10 scale or a mild/medium/hot rating. The heat of a chilli can vary enormously depending on the variety, growing conditions and soil. Everyone tastes things in a different way, so each mouth also has its own scale.

The hotness and burning sensation of a chilli pepper derives from a substance named capsaicin. It is concentrated in the seeds and pith (membrane) surrounding the seeds.

Fresh chillies are green until they ripen. As they ripen, they turn red, yellow, purple, orange or brown. The spectrum of colours is enormous. Some varieties are sold mature and some green.

Ripe chilli peppers are always just as hot as green, but their taste is often slightly sweeter and fuller.

Drying chillies intensifies and strengthens their flavour.

It is often said that the smaller the chilli, the hotter it will be. This rule does not always hold; there is no way to be certain about a chilli until you have tested it yourself. There are many tastes; we are all accustomed to different flavours.

CHIVES

Chives are widely available fresh and are easy to grow in the home garden. They may also be found dried.

They have a mild, oniony flavour.

CLOVES

The clove is one of our oldest spices. The part of the clove tree used as a spice are the flower buds, which are picked before flowering has begun. The buds are dried, at which time they turn hard and dark brown.

According to an Indonesian story, the flowering of a clove tree was a good omen for the children of the family. Children were adorned with clove necklaces, which were believed to protect them from evil spirits.

The aroma is intense, almost burning and slightly peppery.

CINNAMON

Cinnamon is the dried bark of the cinnamon tree. It is sold both as sticks and powdered.

Cinnamon is soothing and aids digestion. It is also a natural antiseptic.

CORIANDER
cilantro (Unites States)
Coriander can be found as seeds or a powder, as well as in fresh herb form. In Thai cuisine, coriander root is used even more that the leaves or seeds. In Europe, however, it is difficult to find the root.

Spices on left side from top: cardamom seed pods, fenugreek and coriander seed. Right side from top: nutmeg, cloves and cumin seed (jeera).

Coriander seeds are one of the most important ingredients in curry and garam masala spice mixtures.

The aroma of fresh coriander is citric and gingery.

Coriander is said to ease joint pain, stomach ache and shortness of breath. In the *Book of One Thousand and One Nights,* coriander is known as an aphrodisiac.

CUMIN

The names jeera and Roman caraway are also used for cumin. Don't confuse cumin with caraway! They are two very different spices.

The connection between the names may have arisen because caraway supplanted the use of cumin in Europe in the Middle Ages.

Cumin was primarily a medicinal plant in ancient Egypt and Crete. However, the Romans learned to use it as a generic spice, just as we use pepper.

At one time, cumin was used in many love potions, because it was believed to improve the faithfulness between lovers.

CURRY LEAVES

Curry leaves come from the tree *Chalcas koenigii,* which grows in Southeast Asia. The scent of curry leaves is aromatic, musky and slightly citric. The taste is pleasantly warm, citric and almost imperceptibly bitter.

Curry leaves are sold dried; fresh leaves are found infrequently. Unfortunately, curry leaves lose their nuanced aroma as they dry.

Curry leaves should not be confused with curry powder, which is a mixture of spices. However, in Asia, curry leaves are often used as part of the curry mixture, especially if the tree happens to be growing in one's own back yard!

CURRY POWDER

Curry is a spice mixture. There are as many different curries in India as there are mothers. The base ingredients in curry are often turmeric, chillies, cumin, black pepper, nutmeg, cloves and coriander. For tips on preparing spice mixtures, see p. 170.

Nota bene! The best aromas and flavours are to be had from a curry mixture by heating it in oil before adding it to the food.

DILL/DILL WEED

Dill belongs to the basic line-up in home gardens in northern climes. The whole herb, including the seeds, is usable.

Dill has an anise-like flavour somewhat reminiscent of parsley. The seeds, on the other hand, are similar both in outward appearance and somewhat in flavour to caraway.

Dill was being used for the alleviation of headaches and other aches and pains as far back as the time of the ancient Egyptians.

FENNEL

The most common form of fennel in the kitchen is fennel seeds. They have a mild flavour reminiscent of anise and liquorice. In Asian cuisine, candied fennel seeds are offered as after dinner sweets.

In India, fennel water is used as an aid in treating colicky babies. It is believed to have healing effects for rheumatism, asthma and tooth and ear aches.

FENUGREEK

Fenugreek belongs to the clover and pea family. Its seeds are small, dark yellow and nearly square.

12

Although Asian cuisine values fenugreek so much that it is an essential part of most curry mixtures, it is still under-appreciated in Europe. This may be a result of the plant's origin. The scientific name of fenugreek is *Trigonella foenum-graecum*. *Trigonella* refers to the odd shape of the flowers and *foenum-graecum* means Greek hay, i.e. fodder for cattle. Or is it a result of Europeans' hesitation due to the fact that fenugreek increases appetite, and Egyptian men even encouraged their wives to eat the seeds, because they were fond of rounded figures.

GALANGAL
Galangal root is similar in appearance to ginger root.

There are two varieties of galangal: greater galangal, which is cultivated in Indonesia and Malaysia, and lesser galangal. These have subtle differences in taste. The flavour of greater galangal is a combination of citrus, ginger and cardamom. Lesser galangal, on the other hand, is more piquant, with the aroma of pepper and eucalyptus.

Although galangal is primarily an Asian spice, its English name originates from the Arabic word *khalanjan*.

In well-stocked shops, galangal may be found fresh, dried, powdered and as a paste. The powdered form is commonly found under the name *Laos powder*.

GARLIC
There is surely no other item in the kitchen that causes so much division than good old garlic. It is loved and hated so much that it has gotten quite a reputation over the years. If vampires or flu are troubling you, magical and undeniably healthy garlic will take care of things!

Garlic may be purchased fresh, dried and also powdered. The flavour of this prince of epicures only strengthens and deepens when dried.

GINGER
Ginger belongs to the same family of spice lilies as turmeric and cardamom. The only part of ginger that is used is the root tuber.

Ginger root may be used fresh or as a dried powder.

Early use of ginger is reported thousands of years ago in Sanskrit literature.

HORSERADISH
Horseradish is a root.

There is something mustardy about horseradish, and it is quite effective in opening up the sinuses. For many, horseradish may indeed bring to mind childhood flu remedies.

Horseradish may be purchased as a fresh root or as a paste.

KAFFIR LIME LEAVES
The Kaffir lime is a lesser known citrus plant. Its fruit is reminiscent of the common lime, but is a rougher, bumpier version. Both the grated rind (zest) of the fruit and the leaves are used in flavouring soups and casseroles.

Most cooks know Kaffir lime by its Thai name *makrut lime*.

LAVENDER
The most beautiful and pure combination of purple and blue colours is to be found in the lavender fields. Lavender does not thrive in very cold climates, but may overrun gardens at latitudes as far north as England.

Lavender is a sweet herb, whose scent is surely known even by those who have never seen the herb in

question. Its unique, spicy-sweet smell calms the nerves and soothes the soul.

Aromatic oils are made from lavender, and its flower can be used intact for its fragrance. It gives a lovely piquant overtone to herb and spice mixtures (p. 174).

LEMON BALM

Lemon balm belongs to the same family as the mints.

Its aromatic leaves entice both cooks and bees, and it is recommended for planting near honey-producing hives.

Lemon balm leaves give off a mellow citric, minty aroma when touched. It is wise to only use fresh leaves from this herb, because older leaves often have a stale taste.

LEMON GRASS

Lemon grass looks more like a reed than an herb. It gets its name from the citric flavour of its stalk.

The flavour of lemon grass is released when the stalk is crushed or ground. The grass is not meant to be eaten, but rather lends itself more to flavouring.

This spice, previously unknown in Europe, has spread to our kitchens only as Indonesian, Thai and Vietnamese cuisine has become more common.

Lemon grass is generally used fresh, dried or powdered. It is also available as a paste.

MANGO POWDER
amchoor

Mango powder is made by powdering dry, unripe mango slices. Mango powder is beautiful sandy brown in colour and slightly sweet and fruity in taste.

Mango powder is a charming acquaintance which has finally reached our shores, although it is generally produce only in India.

The name *amchoor* is a direct loan from Hindi (am-choor).

Mango powder may be found in ethnic food shops, as well as other well-stocked groceries. Mango is also sold dried and sliced.

MARJORAM
OREGANO

Oregano and marjoram are sister herbs. Oregano has a stronger and spicier flavour than marjoram.

The ancient Romans used marjoram as a flavouring in both olive oil and wine. Marjoram has been considered a symbol of honour, and, in their day, the Romans wove wedding garlands out of it for the bride and bridegroom.

MINT
SPEARMINT
PEPPERMINT

There are many different flavours of mint, the best known of which to us are probably *spearmint* and *peppermint*. Peppermint oil, which contains menthol, is extracted from peppermint. However, spearmint is used more in food preparation and is sold both fresh and dried.

MUSTARD

Mustard is the common name for the seeds of several plants of the family Brassicacae (or "crucifers"). Different varieties include yellow mustard seed, which is the common raw ingredient of prepared mustards, and black mustard seed, which is darker in colour.

Yellow mustard seed may also be purchased as a powder, from which it is easy to make mustard itself.

Mustard seeds are used as a component of spice mixtures in eastern cuisine.

Mustard seed was already widely available in Europe by the Middle Ages, because it is a very inexpensive spice.

NUTMEG MACE

Both nutmeg and mace are had from the same tree.

Nutmeg is a large, hard seed. There are even graters developed specifically for the grating of nutmeg. It may be purchased as a powder, but it is wise to buy it whole, so that its deep, woody aroma will be better preserved.

Mace is the red, dried aril, or covering, around the actual nutmeg seed, both of which are contained within an apricot-like fruit.

The flavour of mace is milder than nutmeg.

PAPRIKA

Paprika powder is produced from sweet varieties of the *Capsicum* family cultivated in Europe. It is an essential spice in Hungarian cuisine, but it is also used frequently in Spain.

Paprika powder is easy to use and has a pleasant flavour. It may be purchased in both hot and mild versions.

PARSLEY

Parsley is a popular herb, which is available both fresh and dried.

If you don't know which herb to acquaint yourself with first, start with parsley. It will never let you down.

Curly leaf and Italian, or flat leaf, parsley are the most popular, although root parsley is considered to have a more full flavour.

Parsley is lightly spicy in flavour and it has a pinch of anise and citric aroma.

PEPPERCORNS BLACK PEPPER GREEN PEPPER WHITE PEPPER

Pepper is a vine. Green, black, and white pepper all come from the same plant, but they represent different stages of ripeness of the pepper fruit.

Once pepper was as valuable as gold, and it has remained the king of spices to this day. The Romans even named one of the gates of Alexandria the "Pepper Gate".

Black pepper is the unripe fruit, which is spread in the sun to dry after picking, and dries to a shrivelled black. Its flavour is strongly aromatic and well-rounded.

White pepper comes from the ripe, reddish-yellow fruits. After harvest, the fruits are packed in coarse jute sacks and immersed in flowing water, so that the shells and fruit flesh fall away. After this, the seeds are rinsed and spread in the sun to dry. Green pepper and black pepper are whole fruits, while white pepper is only the seed of the pepper fruit.

Green pepper is also picked unripe. After this, it is freeze-dried or pickled in vinegar or brine.

Green pepper has a slightly milder and more aromatic flavour than the other peppers.

PINK PEPPERCORN

red peppercorn

Pink pepper isn't really pepper, but rather the shiny, small, red fruit of a tropical tree.

The flavour of pink pepper is not terribly strong, but when crushed, its sweetish taste can hold its own.

ROSEMARY

Rosemary (*Rosmarinus officinalis*) is a bush whose leaves are stiff and needle-like. The name rosemary is derived from the Latin

phrase *rosmarinus,* which means "dew of the sea".

The flavour of rosemary is warm, strongly aromatic and very slightly bitter. It also has a barely perceptible hint of pine.

SAFFRON

Saffron is the dried stigmas of the pistil of the saffron crocus. Saffron is known as the world's most expensive spice. And for good reason! 4,000 flowers are needed for 25 grams of saffron.

Saffron may be purchased dried in small amounts from the spice shelf. Sometimes it is also sold as whole stigmas. On journeys abroad, it pays to be careful not to buy turmeric powder in place of saffron. True saffron is always fire red and intensely coloured. Its aroma cannot be mistaken; it has a very strong, honey-like scent. A good way to test the authenticity of saffron is to mix a small amount with water in your hand. If the colouring comes off easily in water, you may have some other plant that has been dyed. The colour of true saffron dissolves slowly.

Despite the expense, it is worthwhile to become acquainted with saffron; it will sweep you off your feet.

SAGE

Sage is a small, fragrant bush, which has small grey-green leaves.

Sage may be purchased as a fresh herb or dried.

The taste of sage is so unique and refined that we recommend using it separately from other spices to do justice to its own flavour.

The name comes from the Latin word *salvere,* which means ´to save´, ´to heal´. Indeed, an old saying inquires: "Why should a man die whilst sage grows in his garden?"

STAR ANISE

There is no way to mistake star anise! It is as beautiful as a flower, a small, star-shaped divine creation. Its aroma is said to bring to mind old fashioned sweet shops, for the aroma combines anise and liquorice.

Star anise is the seed pod of a tree related to the magnolia. It cannot be substituted with anise, for although they are similar spices, they belong to different plant families.

Star anise is well known in Chinese cuisine, especially Cantonese.

Due to its unbelievable aroma, star anise is used as a medicine and as an aromatic essential oil.

THYME

Thyme is a small, herbaceous (stemmed) plant that comes in many varieties. It is often found growing wild. The most common culinary varieties are common thyme (*Thymus vulgaris*) and citrus thyme. Both are easy to grow in the home garden.

Thyme is one of the more fragrant and aromatic of the herbs in the Provence mixtures (p. 174).

In ancient Greece, thyme was considered a symbol of courage and industry. The name is said to have come from the Greek work *thymos,* meaning life force.

TURMERIC

Turmeric is a tropical plant, which belongs to the same spice lily family as ginger and cardamom.

As with ginger, it is the root tuber of turmeric that is used. Turmeric is most commonly found powdered.

Turmeric is characterised by its yellow colour, and indeed, it is generally used in colouring rice dishes. It is also an important part of curry spice mixtures.

In India, one might encounter a holy cow dyed with turmeric, for there, turmeric is used in ritual ceremonies.

VANILLA

Vanilla is the seed pod of a white orchid. Before it is ready for use as a flavouring, it must go through multiple processing steps, which include steaming and alternating dry and wet processing over the space of three or four months. This processing gives vanilla its familiar black, shiny colour and strong scent.

Vanilla - like chocolate - was known during Aztec times and spread to Europe along with the cocoa shipments of the conquering Spanish gourmets. The name vanilla is also a Spanish legacy. It derives from the word *vaina*, which means pod.

Vanilla may be purchase as pods, powdered or as an extract in alcohol solution. It is rather expensive, but worth the price.

Caveat emptor! Imitation vanilla (vanillin) doesn't have anything to do with real vanilla. See how to prepare real vanilla sugar on p. 52.

WASABI

Although wasabi is sometimes called Japanese horseradish in the West, it isn't really horseradish.

Wasabi is a perennial plant of which only the root is used. The root has a burning scent, which makes the nose "tingle"

Wasabi is available as a paste and a powder. The powder may be mixed with warm water to make a paste.

Because genuine wasabi is somewhat expensive, often "faux wasabi" is made by mixing horseradish, mustard and green food colouring. That certainly is another way to open the sinuses.

Wasabi is always enjoyed cold or is added to food only at the end of cooking, because it loses its flavour when heated.

Salads

"I'M WILLING AND ABLE SO I THROW MY CARDS ON YOUR TABLE! SEE: I WANNA LOVE YA, I WANNA LOVE AND TREAT YA – LOVE AND TREAT YA RIGHT. I WANNA LOVE YOU EVERY DAY AND EVERY NIGHT WE'LL BE TOGETHER, WITH A ROOF RIGHT OVER OUR HEADS WE'LL SHARE THE SHELTER OF MY SINGLE BED WE'LL SHARE THE SAME ROOM, YEAH! JAH PROVIDE THE BREAD. WE'LL SHARE THE SHELTER OF MY SINGLE BED."

- BOB MARLEY: IS THIS LOVE

The romantic Protagonist papered his walls, painted his furniture and clothed himself in purple. "Is this your idea of vigorous mental health?" inquired the Authorities. "God knows", pondered the Protagonist, "but this is my production, so be so kind as to allow me to decide myself how to stage it."

Spicy Cinnamon-Bean Salad [PICTURED]

300 ml boiled or canned mixed
  beans red, black and white
3 yellow tomatoes
1–2 tsp finely chopped Habanero
  chillies
1 orange pepper
1 red onion
1 small onion
2 tsp cinnamon
1 tsp raw sugar
juice of 2 limes
½ + ½ tsp fine sea salt

[1] Dice tomatoes. Mince chilli and mix it with
the tomatoes. Sprinkle ½ tsp salt on top and
mix carefully. Allow to marinate for about
half an hour.
[2] Dice pepper and slice onions. Add them to
the tomatoes along with the beans.
[3] Mix the cinnamon, sugar and ½ tsp salt with
the lime juice and pour in with the salad.

Sprout Salad [PICTURED]

400 ml cooked wild rice
200 ml alfalfa sprouts
200 ml mung bean sprouts
1-2 fresh chillies
1 bundle fresh lemon balm
1 red pepper
100 ml peeled pistachios

Mixed green lettuce leaves

[1] Rinse the cooked wild rice and allow it to cool.
[2] Slice the chilli and pepper. Mince the lemon balm leaves.
[3] Mix together all other ingredients except for the lettuce and pistachios.
[4] Assemble the salad such that the green lettuce leaves are placed on the bottom with the other ingredients on top.
[5] Garnish with whole or crushed pistachios. Serve separately or as a side dish with grilled foods.

salads

Gherkin Delight

1 largish cucumber
2 tbsp rice wine vinegar
2 tsp honey or rice syrup
½ + ½ tsp fine sea salt
3 cloves garlic
1 tbsp grated fresh ginger
1 red or green chilli pepper
100 ml fresh coriander, chopped

50 ml toasted sesame seeds

[1] Slice cucumber into largish pieces.
[2] Finely mince garlic cloves and chilli. Grate ginger. Chop coriander.
[3] Mix all ingredients together and allow to rest in a cool place for some time. In the mean time, you can toast the sesame seeds in a dry, hot frying pan. Move the pan back and forth; avoid burning the seeds and only add to salad just before serving.

Chilli Pepper and Noodle Salad

150 g cellophane or rice noodles
2 red onions
2 cloves garlic
2 peppers
2 fresh red chillies
a mix of green lettuce, for example,
   rocket, iceberg lettuce and endive
2 + 2 tbsp olive oil
2 tbsp sesame seeds
2 tsp sesame oil
juice of 2 limes
4 tbsp soy sauce

[1] Boil noodles according to package directions. Drain well and cut into slices about 5 cm long. Let cool.

[2] Cut red onion into slices. Mince garlic and chilli pepper. Remove seeds from pepper and cut into stick-like slices.

[3] Heat 2 tbsp olive oil in a pan and sauté red onion until limp. Add garlic, chilli, pepper and sesame seeds. Sauté quickly for two minutes.

[4] Add lime juice, sesame oil and soy sauce.

[5] Let cool.

[6] Mix noodles and shredded lettuce. Add the fried onion mixture and pour in 2 tbsp olive oil. Serve immediately!

"NEVER EAT MORE THAN YOU CAN LIFT" – MISS PIGGY

Roasted Beetroot Salad

800 g small whole fresh
    beetroot or large, cubed beetroot
3 tbsp vegetable oil
3 peaches
100 g feta cheese
100 ml walnuts

DRESSING

2 tsp sherry vinegar or apple vinegar
2 tsp honey
1 fresh red chilli pepper
3 tbsp olive oil
3 tbsp nut oil
1 tsp sea salt
1 tsp ground black pepper

[1] Heat oven to 180°C.
[2] Clean beetroots with a potato brush and set them in an casserole dish. Sprinkle with oil and cover with tin foil. Bake beetroots 1–1½ hours, until soft.
[3] Let cool and only then peel beets.
[4] Cut peach into large pieces.
[5] Mix dressing: Mix vinegar, honey and minced chilli pepper. Add oils. Season with salt and black pepper.
[6] Pour dressing over peaches and beetroots, but keep them separate at this stage. Otherwise the beetroot will discolour the peaches. Allow the beetroots and peaches to marinate for half an hour.
[7] Arrange beetroots and peaches in a serving dish just before serving. Crumble feta cheese on top and garnish with walnuts.

The sweet flavour of beetroot is brought out by baking in the oven. Savoury feta is a fitting companion for this sweet salad. The chilli dressing gives the salad a kick.

Chèvre
Salad [PICTURED]

1 head green lettuce
10 fresh spinach leaves
200 ml sunflower shoots
1 pack Cape gooseberries (physalis)
2 tsp ground black pepper
50-100 ml roast pumpkin seeds
   or sunflower seeds

4 100 g rounds of chèvre (goat's milk
cheese)

DRESSING

2 tbsp warm water
2 tbsp white wine vinegar or apple
   vinegar
2 tsp honey
1 tbsp Dijon mustard
2 tsp ground pink pepper + a few
   whole for garnish

[1] Prepare salad dressing by mixing all dressing ingredients together with the warm water. Place in a cool spot to rest.
[2] Place lettuce leaves on serving plates. Shred spinach leaves and sprinkle them and the sunflower shoots over the lettuce.
[3] Remove pods from the gooseberries and slice in half.
[4] Grind black pepper over salad and sprinkle on pumpkin seeds.
[5] Sauté goat cheese rounds in a hot pan until brown. Set them on top of the salad while warm.
[6] Pour salad dressing over everything and serve immediately.

Roasted Tomato Salad [PICTURED]

12 medium-sized tomatoes
1 tsp coriander seeds
1 tsp caraway seeds
2 tsp sea salt
2 tsp sugar
100 ml olive oil

DRESSING
1 tsp harissa (p. 174)
1 clove garlic
1 red onion
1 tbsp fresh coriander
juice and grated zest of 1 orange
4 tbsp nut oil

[1] Heat oven to 150°C.
[2] Roast coriander and caraway seeds for a moment in a hot, dry pan.
[3] Halve tomatoes and place them in a casserole dish, cut side up. Sprinkle roasted spices, salt and sugar over them and then sprinkle with olive oil.
[4] Roast tomatoes in oven for about 30 minutes, until they become soft and shrivel slightly.
[5] Prepare dressing: Mince red onion, garlic and coriander leaves. Mix all ingredients and let stand at room temperature until tomatoes are ready.
[6] Place tomatoes on serving dish and pour dressing over them. Serve warm or chilled.

32

Chilled Potato-Chickpea Salad

10 boiled potatoes, chilled
400 g canned chickpeas
   or 200 ml boiled chickpeas
1 red onion
2–3 tbsp olive oil
2 cloves garlic
1 red chilli pepper
3 tsp cumin powder
juice of 1–2 limes

DRESSING

200 ml crème fraîche or soy-based
   crème fraîche

50 ml dried mint
2 tbsp olive oil
½ tsp herb salt
1 tsp ground black pepper

[1] First prepare the dressing and place it in the refrigerator to rest.

[2] If using dried chickpeas, soak them overnight in cold water. Rinse carefully and boil according to pack directions. It is a good idea to boil a larger batch and freeze some for later use.

[3] This delicacy can be whipped up from yesterday's left-over potatoes. Cut up potatoes and mix with chickpeas.

[4] Remove seeds from the chilli pepper and mince.

[5] Heat the oil in a frying pan. Sauté the spices, chilli pepper and onions briefly in the oil. Add the potatoes and chickpeas. Stir the mixture so that the spices are distributed throughout.

[6] Mix in the cold dressing and serve immediately.

Soups

....

"WELL GOODNIGHT MOON
I WANT THE SUN
IF IT'S NOT HERE SOON
I MIGHT BE DONE
NO IT WON'T BE TOO SOON 'TIL
I SAY GOODNIGHT MOON"

SHIVAREE: GOODNIGHT MOON

....

The Man met the Woman's emerald eyes in the morning rush and noticed her creative necklace woven from cardamom pods. Perplexed, the Man dug out of his pocket the cardamom key chain he had made himself. The Woman smiled. She had been waiting for the Man for years. In that moment, the word "fateful" took on new meaning for the Man, and on every morning from then on fell in love with cardamom and its bearer again and again.

Winged Fairy's Lentil Soup

400 ml red lentils
500 g crushed tomatoes
2 carrots
1 leek
2 onions
4 cloves garlic
1 vegetable stock cube
1 tsp sea salt
1 l water
1 fresh red chilli pepper

ALSO

cottage cheese
vegetable oil or butter

[1] Rinse lentils carefully.
[2] Boil the lentils alone at first in order to skim off the foam that will rise to the surface. If you wish, you may change the water in between.
[3] Chop the vegetables and chilli pepper. Add all ingredients to soup.
[4] Boil until carrots are tender. Leave soup to stew for a moment.
[5] Purée soup with a hand blender.
[6] Add cottage cheese to soup before serving.

Walford Gazpacho in Ice Bowl

15 ripe tomatoes (about 800 g)
1 tbsp olive oil
3 cloves garlic
4 spring onions with tops
1 cucumber
1 green pepper
1 yellow pepper
50 ml sweet chilli sauce
juice of 3 limes and grated zest
about 700 ml water
1 tsp fine sea salt
2 tsp ground black pepper

ICE BOWL PREPARATION

You will need:
a large and a small bowl
   water
slices of chilli pepper and lime as garnish

[1] Prepare ice bowl: Pour water into plastic bowl (diameter about 27 cm). Place the smaller bowl (diameter about 22 cm) inside the larger bowl. To keep the smaller bowl in place during freezing, place wide masking tape across the top of the large and small bowls. Add enough water that the space between the bowls fills completely. You can drop small pieces of red chilli pepper and lime slices into the water as garnish. Freeze bowl overnight.

[2] Prepare soup: Scald tomatoes, peel and dice. Dice other ingredients as well. Grate lime zest and squeeze juice.

[3] Heat oil in a pan and sauté spring onions and garlic.

[4] Combine all ingredients and pour cold water over them. Season soup with sweet chilli sauce, lime zest and lime juice, as well as with salt and black pepper. Chill soup in refrigerator.

[5] Remove bowl from freezer just before serving. Pour warm water into the smaller bowl and separate it. Fill the ice bowl with the cold gazpacho.

Roasted Tomato Soup [PICTURED]

15 (about 800 g) extremely ripe
   tomatoes
4 tbsp olive oil
1 large onion
2 cloves garlic
2 tsp cumin powder
1 tsp coriander seeds
1 tbsp paprika
1 tsp minced Habanero chilli
1 tbsp tomato purée
700 ml vegetable stock
4 tbsp dark balsamic vinegar
2 tsp raw sugar
1 tsp sea salt
2 tsp ground black pepper

GARNISH

Cream or soy cream and paprika
   powder

[1] Heat oven to 200°C. Split tomatoes and place in a casserole dish cut side up. Sprinkle half of the olive oil on tomatoes and heat in oven for 20-30 minutes, until tomatoes soften and colour slightly.

[2] Heat the remaining olive oil in a saucepan and add the minced onion and garlic, cumin, coriander and paprika. Sauté briefly, but do not allow to burn.

[3] Add minced chilli pepper, roasted tomatoes and tomato purée to saucepan. Fry on medium heat for about 5 minutes.

[4] Add vegetable stock and bring to a boil. Reduce heat and let simmer covered for two minutes. Mix evenly using hand blender.

[5] Add sugar and balsamic vinegar to soup. Let simmer on medium heat for 3-5 minutes and then set aside to cool. Add the rest of the salt and pepper.

[6] Garnish soup with cream and paprika; serve hot or chilled.

Jumbo Prawn Soup [PICTURED]

8 jumbo prawns
200 g shiitake mushrooms
1 tsp minced Habanero chilli
5 slices galangal root or 1 tsp
  galangal paste
2 stalks lemon grass
700 ml fish stock
3 tbsp Asian fish sauce
juice of 4 limes
2-3 kaffir lime leaves
100 ml minced fresh coriander

[1] Wash and clean jumbo prawns. Shell them, if using whole prawns, but leave the tail, because then they look more attractive.
[2] Cut lemon grass into diagonal slices. Cut five slices of galangal root. Add lemon grass and galangal slices to boiling fish stock and boil until lemon grass becomes soft.
[3] Wash and cut mushrooms in two.
[4] Add jumbo prawns and mushrooms to soup. Let boil on medium heat for about 5 minutes.
[5] Remove seeds from chilli pepper and mince. Add it to the soup with lime juice and fish sauce.
[6] Mince coriander and lime leaves; sprinkle on the surface of the soup. Serve soup steaming hot.

Warm Fish Soup

1 tbsp vegetable oil
2 tbsp grated fresh ginger
1-2 fresh red long chilli peppers
juice of 1 lime and grated zest
1 tbsp brown sugar
700 ml water
1 tsp sea salt
3 carrots
½ kg potatoes
3 spring onions with tops
1 can coconut milk
2 tbsp fish fumet (concentrated stock)
or 1 fish stock cube
approx 300 g white fish fillet, e.g.
   cod, haddock, etc

[1] Finely grate ginger and lime zest. Mince chilli pepper.

[2] Heat oil in saucepan and add ginger, lime zest, chilli pepper and brown sugar. Sauté for a moment.

[3] Add water and heat. If using fish stock cube, add it at this stage.

[4] Peel and slice carrots. Add to soup. Boil for approx 5 min.

[5] Peel and cube potatoes. Add to soup and boil for approx 10 min. Chop and add onions, but save some onion tops for garnish.

[6] Add fumet, coconut milk, lime juice and fish fillets cut into bite-sized pieces. Bring soup to a boil and then remove from heat. Let stew stand covered for 10 minutes. Garnish soup with chopped onion tops just before serving.

Creole
Peanut Soup

1 onion
2 tbsp butter or margarine
2 tsp grated fresh ginger
1 tsp grated nutmeg or
 nutmeg powder
1 l vegetable stock
200 ml peanut butter
100 ml soy cream or cream
100 ml white wine

GARNISH

fresh coriander
crushed peanuts

[1] Mince onion. Heat butter in saucepan and sauté onion.
[2] Grate ginger and nutmeg, adding to saucepan.
[3] Add vegetable stock.
[4] When the soup comes to a boil, add peanut butter. Stir constantly.
[5] Add cream and white wine. Garnish and serve hot.

Coconut
Spinach-Potato Soup

[PICTURED]

8–10 medium-sized potatoes
1 fresh green chilli pepper
300 ml green or brown lentils
1 l water
1 vegetable stock cube
1 onion
4 cloves garlic
2 tsp cumin powder
1 tin (approx 400 g) coconut milk
2 tsp herb salt
50–100 g fresh spinach
1 tsp ground black pepper

[1] Wash potatoes.
[2] Rinse lentils carefully and bring to a boil. Boil for ten minutes and change water. Add vegetable stock cube at this stage.
[3] Remove seeds from chilli pepper and mince. Cube potatoes and onions. Add all ingredients to saucepan except fresh spinach. Boil until potatoes begin to soften.
[4] Let soup stand covered and then shred spinach into soup.
[5] Serve with fresh bread.

THE ITALIAN SON-IN-LAW THOUGHT HIMSELF POSSESSED OF SUPERNATURAL POWERS - AND MUST HAVE SAID HIS PRAYERS THE NIGHT BEFORE - WHEN IN THE MORNING, WINE CAME FROM THE TAP INSTEAD OF WATER. THE AUTHORS OF THE TRICK TURNED OUT TO BE THE COUSINS THAT CAME WITH THE DOWRY, BUT THAT DIDN'T PUT OUT THE SON-IN-LAW. CHEST PUFFED OUT, HE BRAGGED IN THE VILLAGE ABOUT WHAT A GOOD FAMILY HE HAD MARRIED INTO: EVEN THOUGH HIS BRIDE WAS ILL-TEMPERED, HER BROTHERS WERE ANGELS INCARNATE.

Iris's Captivating Cold Soup

Two large or four small servings.

2 slices white bread
4 large tomatoes
2 small fresh green chilli peppers
1 cucumber
1 small leek
2 cloves garlic
100 ml olive oil
1 tsp sea salt
1 tsp caraway seeds
juice of 1 lemon
200 ml cold water

GARNISH
Fresh coriander or
   parsley sprigs

[1] Cut hard crusts from bread. Put bread in a dish with a small amount of water to soften.
[2] Scald and peel tomatoes.
[3] Remove seeds from chilli peppers.
[4] Heat bread in a frying pan to remove water.
[5] Purée all ingredients together in a blender.
[6] Garnish with coriander or parsley sprigs.

Kenian Summer Soup [PICTURED]

approx 2 kg watermelon
2 long fresh red chillies
lemon balm leaves as garnish

ALSO
ice cubes

[1] Cut up watermelon and remove seeds.
[2] Remove seeds from the chilli pepper and mince.
[3] Mix watermelon and chilli pepper in serving bowl. Purée soup with hand blender.
[4] Garnish with lemon balm leaves.
[5] Add ice cubes to soup so that it stays cold longer.

Tips

....

"CAN'T YOU FEEL THAT LOVE IS WAITING"

- KENT: KÄRLEKEN VÄNTAR

....

FRESH CHILLI PEPPERS

Nowadays it is not difficult to find fresh chilli peppers on the market shelf. Fresh chillies are often imported from Asia, but domestically-grown chillies may also be found.

Chillies sold in groceries are often anonymous, being sold under the generic name "chilli pepper" and often without any information about their level of heat. In these situations, the only way to discover the chilli's strength is by experimentation. When you buy chilli peppers, be sure that they are crisp-feeling, shiny skinned and smooth. Also check to make sure they don't have blotches or spots. Store chilli peppers in the refrigerator rolled in kitchen paper so they can breath. They quickly shrivel in plastic bags. A fresh chilli pepper will keep in the refrigerator for about three weeks. If they are left at room temperature, they lose flavour and shrivel quickly.

DRIED CHILLI PEPPERS

When buying dried chillies, ensure that they have good colour and are not dusty. Dried chillies give off a marvellous, pungent aroma upon opening the jar. Keep dried chillies in an air-tight container. However, do not keep them for years at a time; rather, use them within a few months of buying.

HANDLING CHILLI PEPPERS

Chilli peppers can literally burn if you handle them carelessly. Capsaicin, the burning component of chilli peppers, is most concentrated in the seeds and membranes, and also somewhat in the fruit flesh. If you have scrapes on your hands or happen to rub your eyes or mucous membranes after handling a chilli pepper, the burning sensation can be very painful. Even washing well with soap does not remove the burning, and the burning sensation can remain on the skin for several hours. A trip to the sauna is not a good idea with this burning!

Also those with allergies sensitive to smells may have an allergic reaction simply upon entering a room where a hot chilli pepper has been handled. Use thin protective gloves when handling chilli peppers in order to protect your skin. Clean kitchen implements carefully after use.

In some of the recipes in this book, the reader is encouraged to remove the seeds from the chilli peppers. The seeds are hot and by removing them you may control the heat. In addition, the texture of the seeds does not fit well with some of the sweet dishes, but it is only by experimentation that you will be able to determine which seeds fit your taste and mouth.

Leaving out the seeds of a dried chilli pepper does not influence its heat, because the capsaicin has spread through the chilli differently than in a fresh chilli. But in some circumstances, dried seeds may be slightly musty tasting.

Always clean chilli peppers before use. Remove the stems. Split them in two lengthwise and then scoop the seeds out as necessary. You can chop the chillies with a knife or cut them into pieces with scissors.

You can peel chillies (and other peppers) by heating them in a 200-250°C oven for 10 minutes. Afterwards, put the hot chillies

in a plastic bag for fifteen minutes, where the steam will separate the peel. Then you can simply pull the peel off.

If you soak dried chillies in boiling water, they soften and are easier to handle in a mortar when making, for example, chilli paste.

DEALING WITH HEAT IN THE MOUTH

Capsaicin is a fat-soluble compound, so if a chilli burns your mouth, drinking water or beer won't help the matter. There may be different opinions about this in Mexico.

Water just spreads the capsaicin around in the mouth, so try a milk product, for example yoghurt, milk or cheese. Even a piece of bread may relieve the burning in your mouth.

WHY IS IT WORTH EATING CHILLIES?

Chilli peppers are rich in vitamin C. It stimulates appetite, speeds up the metabolism, calms the mind and cools the body, especially in hot conditions.

FREEZING

If you do not have fresh chilli peppers available year-round, the freezer is your best friend. It is a good idea to freeze soft herbs such as basil, parsley and marjoram, which are difficult to dry.

Mince the herbs and mix them with a small amount of water or oil. Freeze the herbs in ice cube trays or small ramekins. In the same way you can also freeze your own chilli paste. Herbs keep in the freezer for 3–4 months.

DRYING

It is easy to dry herbs, but drying does not work for all herbs. It is appropriate for herbs with a woody stem and thick leaves, such as thyme, oregano, rosemary and sage.

Tie the herbs in small bunches and hang them in an airy, shaded spot. It is most handy to dry herbs in a dehydrator. Dried herbs are ready when the leaves crumble between your fingers. Remove the leaves from the stem and keep them in an air-tight container away from light.

HERB AND SPICE BUTTERS

Delicious herb butter mixtures can be made from several herbs. You can also combine spice mixtures with butter, giving it, for example, an eastern zing. Use unsalted butter for spice butters because spice mixtures generally already contain salt.

Mix room-temperature butter and herbs or spices with a wooden spoon or fork. Spread the butter mixture on clingfilm and form it into a block. Keep the butter in the refrigerator or freezer. It is easier to cut the blocks when frozen. Serve with e.g. grilled foods.

SPICE OILS AND VINEGARS

Home-made spice oils and vinegars are easy to prepare and a beautiful housewarming present or gift for a friend.

We recommend the use of basil, dill, garlic, lavender, lemon and rosemary with vinegars. The best spices for vinegars are chilli peppers and coriander or mustard seeds.

For making spiced oils, try bay leaves, basil, garlic, mint, oregano, chilli peppers, anise or dill.

Use 60 g of herbs or spices per ½ litre of oil or vinegar. Mix your desired ingredients in a largish glass jar and seal with an air-tight lid. Let marinate for a few weeks. The flavours come out more quickly if you store the vinegar container in the sun. However, oil must be stored away from the sun. When the flavours have infused the liquid, you can bottle the oil or vinegar in small, clean serving bottles corked air-tight.

Spiced vinegars last for several years unopened, but spiced oils only last about one year. Store both in a dark, cool place or in the refrigerator. Once opened, they should be used as quickly as possible.

VANILLA

Vanilla pots ought not be thrown out after use. They are recycling at its best. Money invested in vanilla pods is money well spent!

VANILLA SUGAR

The best vanilla sugar in the world is had by making it yourself. This delicacy is also a beautiful and delicious gift packaged in a glass jar. Nota bene! Vanillin sugar doesn't have anything to do with vanilla sugar.

Easy Vanilla Sugar

Caster sugar
A few used vanilla pods

Store the vanilla pods and raw sugar in an air-tight container. Voilà, marvelously aromatic sugar!

Gourmet-style Vanilla Sugar

Caster sugar
A few used vanilla pods

[1] After using the seeds from a vanilla pod, you can still use the pods.
[2] Grind the dried vanilla pods and sugar finely in a liquidiser.
[3] If you wish, you can sift the resulting mixture.
[4] Store this delicacy in an air-tight container.

Vanilla Tea

Black or green tea leaves
Used vanilla pod

Chop the vanilla pod with scissors and mix with tea leaves. You will get the best results if you have the patience to allow the mixture to rest in a cool place for two or three weeks.

Vanilla Syrup

This American delicacy deserves a place in our kitchens as well. An unbeatable combination with pancakes or crepes! Try different variations, for example mixing with fresh fruits or berries.

300-400 ml maple syrup
2 used vanilla pods

Heat the syrup and pods in a frying pan. Bring to a slow boil for a moment. Store the syrup in the refrigerator – if there is a drop left over!

Vegetable Dishes

··

"COLOURS OF THE WORLD
SPICE UP YOUR LIFE
EVERY BOY AND EVERY GIRL
SPICE UP YOUR LIFE
PEOPLE OF THE WORLD
SPICE UP YOUR LIFE"

– SPICE GIRLS: SPICE UP YOUR LIFE

··

The unsuspecting Greengrocer ripped off the top of the banana crate, as he had done on a thousand previous mornings. The stowaway Snake did not appreciate the violent wake-up call. As the Greengrocer lay in the poison treatment centre as an extension to a drip tube, his life flashed before his eyes. But not as an elegant continuum like in a film. Strange, random snatches filled his retinas: a casual girlfriend's orthodontics, a history teacher's hairnet, the red ink that stained a Sunday shirt, an unpaid phone bill, his mother's dimples, the bicycle that ended the promising beginnings of his career as an Iron Man and so forth. The Snake's victim considered his life. Were these the highlights? Was this a life worth living? Before the last drops of the bottle fell, he was convinced that this must be the case. On the following mornings of his life, he opened banana crates respectfully. How can you know in which box A New Life is lurking!

Kimchi

1 Chinese cabbage
50 g sea salt

½ leek
2 red onions
1 carrot
4 cloves garlic
1 tbsp grated fresh horseradish
1 tbsp grated fresh ginger
2 red chilli peppers
200 g radish
500-600 ml cold water
1 tbsp sugar
1-2 tsp cayenne pepper

[1] Remove hard core from the cabbage. Cut the cabbage into strips about 5 cm long.
[2] Arrange the cabbage strips in a clean dish, layering with salt. Place a weight on the dish such that the cabbage is pressed by the weight. Leave in the refrigerator for one or two days.
[3] Rinse the cabbage and squeeze out any excess water. Put the cabbage in a clean container.
[4] Cut the leek, red onion, carrot and radishes into thin strips and mix them with the cabbage.
[5] Mince chilli pepper and garlic. Grate horseradish and ginger. Mix remaining ingredients with cabbage.
[6] Mix cold water, sugar and cayenne pepper separately and then add to cabbage mixture. Keep cabbage mixture in the refrigerator covered for one more night before serving. Serve kimchi with warm rice, for example.

Korean cuisine loves chillies and peppers! Nature, harmony, combining and sharing are the key words in Korean culinary culture.

Kimchi is the Korean national food, which is prepared much like sauerkraut. The most important raw ingredient is Chinese cabbage, which is soaked in salt overnight.

vegetable dishes

Spicy Beans
to Remember

200 ml dried azuki beans
200 ml dried black-eyed beans
100 ml dried navy beans
   or a total of 2–3 tins canned beans

DRESSING

3 tbsp grated fresh ginger
3 cloves garlic
1 largish onion
2 tbsp sunflower oil
2 fresh red chilli pepper or 1½ tsp
  minced habanero
½ tsp cayenne pepper
2 tbsp cumin seeds
1½ tbsp coriander seeds
2 tsp turmeric powder
150 ml water
juice of ½ lemon
a handful of fresh coriander

[1] Set the beans to soaking the night before. You can also use canned beans, but not all of the beans used in this recipe are available canned. This mixture of beans yields a delicious combination, so the small bother is worth it.

[2] Drain the beans and replace cooking water. Cook beans according to pack directions (generally about an hour).

Prepare the dressing while the beans are boiling:

[3] Grate the ginger and mince the garlic and onion.

[4] Split the chilli pepper and remove the seeds. Mince the chilli pepper.

[5] Heat oil and sauté the chilli pepper, ginger and onion until soft.

[6] Grind the cumin and coriander seeds carefully with a spice mill or mortar.

[7] Add all of the spices to the pan and stir continuously. Allow the spices to "open up" for a few minutes.

[8] Add the water and lemon juice to the spices. Chop and add the coriander. Let boil for 5–10 min.

[9] When the beans are ready, drain them carefully and rinse under cold water. Add the beans to the food and let simmer for 10 min. If using canned beans, it is a good idea to drain them before adding.

[10] Serve with Colourful Rice (p. 70).

[11] If any food is left over, it can be frozen immediately or used on the following day in a casserole. The flavour will only improve!

Marvellous
Moroccan Couscous

250 ml couscous
3 tbsp olive oil
½ tsp sea salt
500 ml boiling water
1 red pepper
2-3 carrots
1 courgette
2 onions

SAUCE

2 tbsp tomato purée
1 tbsp olive oil
1 tsp sea salt
2 crushed cloves garlic
½ tsp ground black pepper
2 tsp harissa (p. 174)

[1] Prepare sauce by mixing ingredients together.
[2] Slice vegetables. Mix other vegetables except onion with sauce.
[3] Heat oil in a large saucepan or pot. Add sliced onions. Add couscous. Fry couscous in oil until golden yellow.
[4] Add the rest of the vegetables and sauce.
[5] Add boiling water and salt. Turn off heat and let couscous cook covered for about 15 minutes.

If you wish to make this meal more filling, you can use unflavoured tofu or chicken in addition to the vegetables. If doing so, marinate the tofu or chicken in the sauce ahead of time and add it to the couscous with the veggies. Tofu need not be cooked separately, but meat must be cooked, e.g. by stir-frying.

60

Crescent Inn
Bean Casserole

1 red onion
2 cloves garlic
1 tbsp tandoori masala spice mixture
  (p. 171)
2 tbsp vegetable oil
400 g or 300 ml pre-cooked or
  canned red (kidney) beans
400 g crushed tomatoes
1 packet (250 g) Halloumi cheese

FOR SERVING

red rice

[1] Chop onion.
[2] Heat the oil in a pan and add the tandoori masala powder. Stir for a moment so the spice will "open up" and add the onions. Sauté.
[3] Add tomatoes and beans. Let simmer for about 15 minutes.
[4] Cube Halloumi and add.
[5] Serve with cooked rice.

Alex's Quesadillas

8 tortillas
16 slices cheddar cheese or
  soy-based cheddar cheese slices

PASTE

50 ml pitted Kalamata olives
3 tsp green chilli paste (p. 179) or
  1 fresh whole chilli pepper
a few sprigs of fresh parsley
1 tbsp olive oil

FOR BAKING

olive oil

[1] If using fresh chilli pepper, remove the seeds.
[2] Mix paste ingredients with a liquidiser or hand blender.
[3] Heat oven to 180°C.
[4] Spread paste on four tortillas and add four slices of cheddar to each tortilla. Place remaining tortillas on top. Finally, oil with olive oil and bake in oven for 7 minutes.

Kia's Chickpea Curry

300 ml cooked or canned chickpeas

2 large cooked potatoes
1 tsp sea salt
1 tbsp vegetable oil
1 onion
2 tsp grated fresh ginger
1 tsp mango powder
1 tsp cumin powder
1 tsp coriander seeds
2 whole cloves
1 tsp cinnamon powder
½ tsp ground cardamom
1 small dried chilli pepper
fresh coriander

[1] Thinly slice onion. Saute onion slices and grated ginger in oil for a few minutes.
[2] Cut potatoes into cubes and add to the pan. Also add the chickpeas and sprinkle mango powder top. Allow the mixture to heat and cook for a moment. Remove from heat.
[3] Briefly cook the cumin, coriander seeds, cloves, cinnamon, cardamom and crushed chillies in a hot, dry pan.
[4] Grind the spices in a spice mill or mortar. Pour the spices in with the chickpeas. Garnish with fresh coriander.

The mango powder used in this recipe is a fun and interesting new addition to your spice cupboard! It may be found in well-stocked markets and shops specialising in eastern foods and spices.

vegetable dishes

Peppery
Pia's Pizza

DOUGH

200 ml lukewarm water
15-20 g fresh yeast
½ tsp sea salt
1 tsp raw sugar
400-500 ml wheat flour or 500 ml rice
 flour
3 tbsp olive oil

HOT TOMATO SAUCE

200 ml tomato sauce
3 tbsp tomato purée
2 cloves garlic
1 tsp cayenne pepper
2 tsp oregano
¼ tsp sea salt
½ tsp sugar
1 tsp ground black pepper

TOPPING SUGGESTION 1

3-4 tomatoes, sliced
2 red chilli peppers, chopped
8-15 Kalamata olives, sliced
8 sun-dried tomatoes, chopped
½ courgette, sliced thinly
300-400 ml Emmental cheese, grated

TOPPING SUGGESTION 2

1 can sliced mushrooms
1 can pineapple chunks, drained
pepperoni slices
1 red pepper, sliced as circles
1 tsp lemon pepper
300-400 ml cheddar cheese, grated

[1] Heat oven to 250°C.
[2] Crumble yeast into lukewarm water. Add dry ingredients and knead dough for about 10-15 until smooth and elastic. Add olive oil. Leave dough to rise for half an hour in a warm spot.
[3] While dough is rising, prepare tomato sauce. Crush garlic clove and mix all sauce ingredients together.
[4] Roll out crust and set it on a baking sheet covered with baking paper.
[5] Spread tomato sauce and sliced toppings on dough.
[6] Bake the pizza until the crust is ready - depending on the flour for 15-20 min.

Caraway Potatoes

700 g (about 800 ml) mashed potato
  (pre-salted)
1 bunch (about 5) spring onions
  with stalks
2 tbsp vegetable oil
2 tsp caraway seeds
2 tbsp fresh coriander
1 tsp ground black pepper
½ tsp saffron
½ tsp turmeric powder
100 ml cornflour

VEGETABLE OIL

for frying

[1] Chop spring onions with stalks. Sauté them in vegetable oil for a moment and add caraway seeds.

[2] Add onion mixture to the mashed potatoes. Add the rest of the spices and mix well. Let mashed potatoes cool.

[3] Form 8 small, flat circles out of the mash and roll them in the cornflour.

[4] Heat the oil in a pan and fry the potato discs on both sides for about three minutes, until they turn a beautiful golden colour.

[5] Serve potato rounds with salsa made with fresh tomatoes, red onions and chillies (p. 146).

If you happen to have mashed potatoes left over in the refrigerator, use them for this, because they will be nice and sticky and you won't need egg to hold it together.

Mexico Omelette

2 servings

4 organic eggs
½ tsp salt
1 tbsp butter or margarine for frying
1 spring onion
1 mild green chilli pepper
2 tbsp maize
100 g cheddar cheese
½ avocado

[1] Mince onion. Slice chilli pepper and remove seeds. Grate cheese and slice avocado.
[2] Beat eggs lightly and add salt. Pour the egg mixture into a hot pan and fry on medium heat, until the omelette separates at the edges, no longer sticking to the pan. In a non-stick pan you can leave out the butter.
[3] Sprinkle onion, chillies and grated cheese on the uncooked surface. When the cheese has melted, add the avocados and fold the omelette. Serve immediately, for example with green salad.

Mint-Courgette Pancakes

about 18 cakes

500 g grated courgette
½ tsp fine sea salt

5 spring onions
130 g feta cheese
100 ml fresh chopped parsley
100 ml fresh chopped mint
1 tsp ground black pepper
2 organic eggs
150 ml flour (60 g)
 or 200 ml rice flour
olive oil for frying

FOR SERVING
rice
lime slices

[1] Grate courgette coarsely. Sprinkle with sea salt, mix and let rest for about 30 minutes.
[2] Squeeze excess liquid from courgette and dab with kitchen paper.
[3] Mince spring onion and herbs. Crumble feta cheese and add all ingredients to courgette. Season with black pepper.
[4] Place mixture in hot, oiled pan. Fry on both sides for 2 minutes, until the pancakes colour nicely.

vegetable dishes

Baked Lemon Sweet Potatoes

[PICTURED]

½ kg small potatoes
½ kg sweet potatoes

DRESSING
50 ml olive oil
juice and grated zest of 3 limes
2 tsp coarse sea salt
2 tsp crushed black pepper

GARNISH
plenty of fresh lemon balm

[1] Peel and cube sweet potato. Clean potatoes carefully. Do not peel; simply cut in two.
[2] Heat oven to 200°C.
[3] Arrange potato halves and sweet potato cubes in casserole dish.
[4] Prepare dressing and pour it over the potatoes and sweet potatoes.
[5] Bake in oven for about 30 minutes.
[6] Chop lemon balm and mix it in.

Perfect Potatoes

6–10 potatoes

DRESSING
150 ml crème fraîche or soy-based crème fraîche
2 fresh dill sprigs
½ tsp herb salt
¼–½ tsp cayenne pepper
1 tsp wasabi paste

grated cheese, for example Emmental cheese
olive oil for casserole dish

[1] Boil potatoes and cut in half.
[2] Mix dressing: Purée dressing ingredients together and then add chopped dill.
[3] Sprinkle olive oil on the bottom and sides of the casserole dish so the potatoes don't stick to the dish. Arrange potatoes in a single layer. Pour dressing over potatoes. Grate cheese on top.
[4] Bake in oven at 200°C for 15–20 min.
[5] Serve with salmon (p. 104).

vegetable dishes

Colourful Rice

300 ml whole grain rice or basmati rice
3 tbsp olive oil
1 onion
3 cloves garlic
700 ml water
1 low sodium vegetable stock cube
½ tsp sea salt
2 tsp curry spice mixture (p. 170)
200 ml maize
½ red pepper
1 carrot
fresh parsley

[1] Wash rice carefully and leave in sieve to drain.
[2] Chop onions.
[3] Heat olive oil in saucepan and sauté onions.
[4] Add rinsed rice and mix in chopped onions. Sauté for a moment, stirring constantly.
[5] Add water, salt and curry. Crumble in vegetable stock cube.
[6] Let boil for about half of the normal cooking time of the rice. Then simmer for the rest of the time on medium heat. Mix occasionally.
[7] Chop pepper and thinly slice carrot.
[8] Combine pepper, carrot, maize and rice. Mix well and serve immediately. Garnish with parsley.

Wasabi Mashed Potatoes

1 kg floury potatoes
150 g butter or margarine
300 ml hot milk or soy milk
2 tbsp wasabi paste
2 tsp salt

[1] Peel and boil potatoes.
[2] Mash potatoes. Mix in butter or margarine.
[3] Whisk wasabi paste and salt into the hot milk and pour in with mashed potatoes.

Meg's Nutty Mashed Potatoes

1 kg floury potatoes
150 g butter or margarine
300 ml hot milk or soy milk
3 tsp grated nutmeg
2 tsp salt

[1] Peel and boil potatoes.
[2] Mash potatoes. Mix in butter or margarine.
[3] If using whole nutmeg, grate it into hot milk. If using powder, mix it into the milk. Add salt and pour milk mixture in with mashed potatoes.

Grilled Halloumi Skewers with Sunny Sauce [PICTURED]

DRESSING

400 g crushed tomatoes
200 g sun-dried tomatoes
1 tsp sea salt
1 tbsp ground cinnamon
1 tsp ground black pepper

SKEWERS

2 packages Halloumi cheese
skewers for grilling

[1] Mix all dressing ingredients in a liquidiser and season with ground black pepper.
[2] Cut Halloumi cheese in half horizontally and then into four pieces lengthwise. This will give you 8 oblong pieces of cheese that can easily be pushed onto the skewers. Grill skewers until nicely browned. You can also bake the cheese in an oven or fry in a pan. Serve with tomato sauce.

Mother-in-law's Courgette Patties

1 medium courgette
2 tsp sea salt
1 tbsp tandoori masala spice mixture
  (p. 171)
1 tsp herb salt
1 tsp ground black pepper
olive oil

[1] Cut courgette into 1½ cm thick "patties".
[2] "drain" patties: Sprinkle sea salt on patties. Allow to "drain" for about half an hour. You will notice that beads of liquid appear on the surface of the courgette. Rinse the patties under running water and dry with kitchen paper.
[3] Heat the olive oil in a frying pan. Fry patties on both sides until brown.
[4] Dab excess oil from patties with kitchen paper and sprinkle with spices.

Splendid Rice Casserole

1 courgette or aubergine
olive oil
4 cloves garlic
1 tsp curry spice mixture (p. 170)
1 can (400 g) chopped tomato
1 tsp balsamic vinegar
1 tsp honey or ½ tsp sugar
300 ml fresh basil or 3 tbsp dry
   basil
250 ml risotto rice
1 pack (about 250 g) cheddar cheese
or
   Halloumi
100 ml grated Parmesan
2 tsp sea salt
2 tsp ground black pepper
bread crumbs to sprinkle in casserole

[1] Cut courgette or aubergine lengthwise into thin slices. Heat grilling pan or frying pan.

[2] Splash some olive oil on a plate and oil courgette slices. Fry in pan immediately on both sides.

[3] Remove slices and let cool on plate. Pour remainder of frying oil into saucepan, adding a little oil if necessary. Chop garlic and sauté. Add chopped tomatoes, vinegar and spices. Cook for a moment and add chopped basil.

[4] Cook risotto rice in another saucepan until almost done and then add tomato sauce.

[5] Chop chedder cheese or Halloumi into small cubes and grate Parmesan. Mix cheeses with rice mixture. Check salt.

[6] Oil a high-sided bread pan and sprinkle with bread crumbs.

[7] Ladle half of the rice mixture into the bread pan. Set the courgette slices in the pan and fill the rest of the pan with rice mixture. Sprinkle the rest of the broad crumbs on top.

Bake at 220°C for 35 min. Let the dish rest a little and cool off and then tip it upside down on a plate. Cut the rice casserole into serving-sized pieces.

Although this rice casserole is essentially a side dish, in never fails to draw attention away from the entree, it is such a delicacy. If you want to serve this rice casserole as an entree, you can make it into a whole meal by adding a salad.

Meat Dishes

"WHERE HAVE YOU BEEN?
WHERE ARE YOU GOING TO?
I WANT TO KNOW WHAT IS NEW
I WANT TO GO WITH YOU"

- CHRIS REA: THE BLUE CAFE

A bankrupt Businessman was looking for a new direction in his life. At his friends' suggestion he went to an auction with his eye on a glamorous career as an art dealer. A string of events that started with the umbrella of a belligerent granny culminated in what the Businessman took as an unfortunate result. He had unwittingly bid for himself a box full of rusty cans and a stone mortar. The auctioneer was pitiless in the face of his remonstrances: "You should be more specific about what you want. And besides that, there aren't any wrongs, just hidden blessings." At home, holding back her laughter, the Businessman's wife cleaned the tins to while away the time. The Businessman vented his frustration on the mortar. At the same moment they both smelled their new path. The scent of old cinnamon wafted from the mortar and the tins revealed their secrets. In the popular cafe of their spice shop, the Businessman told his listeners over a cup of cinnamon cocoa that, "there aren't mistakes, just blessings in disguise".

Saag Mutton Stew
[PICTURED]

1 kg cubed mutton
1 tbsp vegetable oil
2 tbsp margarine
4 onions
3 cloves garlic
1 tsp turmeric powder
1 tbsp grated ginger
3 cardamom pods
2 tsp cinnamon
100 ml normal fat plain yoghurt
  or plain soy yoghurt
1 tsp fine sea salt
200 ml cold water
400 ml chopped spinach, for example
  frozen spinach
2 tomatoes

[1] Grate onions and crush garlic.

[2] Heat the oil and margarine in a thick-bottomed pot. Sauté the grated onion, crushed garlic, turmeric, grated ginger, cardamom pods and cinnamon until their lovely aroma fills the kitchen. Add meat cubes and salt. Let the meat brown for a moment. Add yoghurt. The more fatty the yoghurt you use, the better it will stand up to heating. Organic Turkish yoghurt is especially well-suited for this use.

[3] Dice tomatoes. Add tomatoes, water and spinach to sauce. Simmer covered or place pot in 170°C oven for an hour. When the meat is cooked through and soft, serve with boiled rice and bread. This delicacy is best on the second day, so if you have the patience, always prepare it a day in advance.

Thai Meatballs in Coconut Sauce

500 g minced white meat, e.g.
  pork or chicken
4 tbsp sweet chilli sauce
2 tbsp Asian fish sauce
2 cloves garlic
1 tsp salt
1 tsp ground black pepper
2 tbsp green curry paste (p. 179)

FOR BOILING

1 l water

SAUCE

1 red pepper
2 carrots
1 tbsp vegetable oil
2 tbsp green curry paste
1 can coconut milk
1 tsp salt

FOR SERVING

Noodles and fresh coriander

[1] Mix minced meat and sweet chilli sauce, fish sauce and minced garlic. Form into small balls.
[2] Boil the litre of water and add the meatballs to the boiling water and cook for about 4 minutes. When they are cooked through, remove from the water with a slotted spoon.
[3] Mix sauce. Slice pepper and carrot thinly. Sauté them for a moment in a hot pan in oil and curry paste. Add coconut milk and salt. Bring to a boil. Add meatballs to sauce.
[4] Boil noodles and serve with sauce. Garnish with fresh coriander.

80

Orange Chicken with Chilli-chocolate Sauce

4 chicken breasts
juice of two oranges
1 tsp whole black peppercorns
1 tsp whole green peppercorns
1 tsp whole pink peppercorns

SAUCE

200 ml prepared demi glace sauce
   base
100 ml port
2 tsp whole black peppercorns
50 g dark chilli chocolate
   (for example Plamil, which is 70%
   cocoa)
1 tsp salt

OR

1 fresh red chilli pepper, if using
   normal dark chocolate

First prepare the sauce:
[1] Simmer the sauce base, port and peppercorns on medium heat for 5-10 min.
[2] Strain out peppercorns.
[3] Grate chocolate. Mix the grated chocolate with the warm sauce. Salt to taste.
[4] If using normal dark chocolate, remove seeds from the chilli pepper, mince it and add to sauce.
[5] Heat the frying pan and squeeze the juice of one of the oranges into the pan. When the juice boils, add the chicken breast fillets to the pan and cook over medium heat. Turn the fillets and when nearly done add the rest of the orange juice.
[6] Crush the peppercorns in a mortar and rub the spice mixture into the surface of the warm chicken fillets. Serve immediately with chocolate sauce.

Satay Pork

500 g pork tenderloin

MARINADE

200 ml coconut milk
1 tsp finely minced galangal root
1 tbsp finely minced lemon grass
2 tsp turmeric powder
2 tsp coriander seeds
½ tsp cumin seeds
½ tsp ground black pepper
1 tsp salt
2 tsp sugar

skewers

SATAY SAUCE

50 ml Omar's Curry Paste (p. 177)
1 can coconut milk
150 ml peanuts
3 tbsp sugar
2 tsp salt (1 tsp if using
   salted peanuts)
50 ml soy sauce

[1] Mix satay sauce: crush peanuts in a mortar or liquidiser. Mix them with the red curry paste.
[2] Heat half of the coconut milk to boiling, add curry-peanut mixture and mix well. Reduce heat and add the rest of the coconut milk. Continue stirring and add sugar, salt and soy sauce. When the mixture thickens, remove from heat and allow to cool.
[3] Prepare meat: First cut pork tenderloin in half crosswise. Then cut halves in half again lengthwise twice so that you are left with 8 long fillets, which will be easy to skewer.
[4] Prepare marinade for meat: Roast coriander and cumin seeds for a moment in a dry pan. Mix all ingredients together, add meat and marinate for at least an hour.
[5] Push meat onto skewers and bake in 200°C oven for about 20 min. Brush them with marinade from time to time.
[6] Serve with satay sauce.

Minced Chicken Skewers and Nutty Ginger Sauce

500 g minced chicken
8 lemon grass stalks as skewers
½ tsp cumin
½ tsp turmeric powder
1 clove garlic
1 tbsp minced fresh ginger
3 spring onions
2 tsp dark sugar (e.g. demerara)
  or dark syrup
5 tbsp vegetable oil
1 tbsp sesame oil
2 tsp Thai fish sauce

PEANUT GINGER SAUCE

300 ml chicken stock
2 tsp Omar's Curry Paste (p. 177)
1 clove garlic
1 red jalapeño
1 tsp honey
1 tbsp grated ginger
6 tbsp peanut butter
1 tsp soy sauce

[1] Mix all ingredients besides minced chicken and lemon grass into a paste using a liquidiser.

[2] Pour paste in with the minced meat and mix well with a wooden spoon. Cover the container with clingfilm and let rest in refrigerator for two hours.

[3] Mix dressing in the meantime: Finely mince garlic and jalapeño. Bring all ingredients to a boil. Move paste to a serving dish and let cool.

[4] Continue preparing skewers. Peel outer layer from lemon grass stalks. Wet hands with warm water and form meat mixture into 8 skewers around lemon grass stalks. Squeeze mixture firmly so that it stays together.

[5] Grill skewers in a hot grill or 200°C oven for about 10-15 min. Serve with peanut ginger sauce.

"UNAUTHORIZED USE", BELLOWED THE EXPERIENCED WINE AFICIONADO TO HIS WIFE, WHO WAS USING A VINTAGE WINE BOTTLE TO MASH POTATOES.

Fruity Curry Beef Gravy

500 g minced beef or 400 ml boiled
   textured soy protein
2 tbsp curry paste (choose your
   favourite: p. 177-179)
1 tbsp vegetable oil
400 ml tomato sauce or prepared
   tomato soup.
200 ml water
1 tsp salt
1 tin (approx 400 g) canned peaches
1 tin (approx 400 g) canned mango
1 banana
100 ml shredded coconut
100 ml peanuts

FOR SERVING
basmati rice

[1] Sauté curry paste in oil in a pan, until the aroma is released.
[2] Add minced meat and brown. When using soy protein, remember to drain well before frying. Pour tomato sauce, water and salt into pan. Let boil on medium heat for about 30 minutes.
[3] Cube peaches and mango, adding them to the gravy. Cube banana and add it carefully. Finally add the peanuts and shredded coconut. Serve immediately with basmati rice.

Exotic Meatballs

500 g minced meat (pork or beef)
1 package onion soup mix
1 package sour cream or 200 ml soft
   tofu
1 tbsp grated fresh ginger
1 tbsp chopped coriander leaves
2 small dried chilli peppers

[1] Remove seeds from chilli peppers and mince.
[2] Mix sour cream with onion soup mix, chopped coriander, grated ginger and minced chillies. Let soak for a moment.
[3] Mix sour cream mixture with minced meat. Finally add egg and mix well.
[4] Roll meat into balls and set on baking paper on a baking sheet.
[5] Bake meatballs in a 175°C oven for about 20 min., depending on the size of the meatballs.

meat dishes

Yoghurt Marinated Turkey Skewers with Spicy Rice

4 turkey breast fillets

MARINADE

400 ml normal fat plain yoghurt
   or soy yoghurt
2 tbsp curry
1 tbsp cumin
1 tsp turmeric powder
2 tsp cinnamon powder
1 tsp harissa (p. 174)
2 tbsp grated fresh ginger

FOR SERVING

rice
1–2 tsp cayenne pepper for rice
   cooking water
skewers

[1] Cut turkey breast fillets in two or three pieces lengthwise. Mix marinade ingredients and add fillets. Let marinate over night in the refrigerator.

[2] Soak wooden skewers in water before use to prevent them burning in the grill.

[3] Skewer turkey fillets and grill until done. Baste them a few times with marinade while grilling.

[4] Serve with cooked rice.

Bulgogi

700 g beef sirloin

MARINADE

150 ml soy sauce
½ of one leek
3-5 cloves of garlic
2 tsp ground black pepper
3 tsp grated fresh ginger
1 long red chilli pepper
1 mild green chilli pepper
2 tsp raw sugar
1 tbsp rice wine vinegar
2 tbsp sesame seeds
1 tbsp sesame oil

DIPPING SAUCE FOR COOKED MEAT

100 ml soy sauce
100 ml water
2 tbsp rice wine vinegar
2 spring onions with stalks, minced

2 cloves garlic, minced
3 tsp sesame seeds

Mix sauce ingredients together.

[1] Slice meat into extremely thin slices. To make cutting easier, you can put the meat in the freezer for a few hours until it hardens.

[2] Prepare marinade: Chop leek, garlic and chilli peppers. Finally, mix all ingredients together and add the thin slices of meat. Let marinate overnight or for at least one hour.

[3] Cook the meat at the table with a table-top home grill such as a raclette grill. Place the meat on the grill with chopsticks and then dip it in the dipping sauce. Good side dishes include rice and kimchi (see p. 56).

Seafood

....

"I UNDERSTAND I'D PROBABLY BE
JUST AS CRAZY ABOUT YOU IF YOU
WERE MY OWN MAN MAYBE NEXT
LIFETIME POSSIBLY UNTIL THEN,
OH FRIEND YOUR SECRET IS SAFE
WITH ME"

- PUSSYCAT DOLLS: DON'T CHA

....

The Prop Manager had given himself over so completely to his obsessive compulsiveness that he had come down with a worsening case of nit-picker's syndrome. His daily routine reached its climax at precisely 2 PM when he took his co-workers to task for a prop shelf being 5 centimetres askew and possibly ushering in the end of the world. And of course the apocalypse came, and naturally in the form of a proproom shelf. As he sprawled beneath the fallen shelf and props, the Prop Manager had a flash of understanding: "If this was unavoidable no matter what, could I have spent the intervening time in a more pleasant manner?"

Fish Patties with Sweet Chilli Sauce

Makes about 12 fish patties

50 ml bread crumbs
100 ml water
10 kaffir lime leaves
1 pepper
1 fresh red chilli pepper
500 g boneless, skinless white fish
    fillet
1 tsp fine sea salt
2 tbsp vegetable oil
2 tbsp buttery margarine

SAUCE
200 ml sweet chilli sauce
50 ml soy sauce

FOR SERVING
jasmine rice

[1] Mix bread crumbs with water. Let soak for about 10 minutes.

[2] Fold lime leaves in half and remove the centre vein. Cut leaves into thin slices.

[3] Slice the pepper and chilli.

[4] Mince fish fillet and mix in pepper, chilli pepper and salt.

[5] Mix bread crumbs and lime leaf slices in with fish.

[6] Form minced fish into 12 thin fish patties and fry them in a pan in a mixture of butter and oil until brown, about 3 minutes on both sides.

[7] Prepare sauce: mix sweet chilli sauce and soy sauce together. Serve fish patties with sauce and jasmine rice.

Spicy Fish in Yoghurt

1 kg white fish fillets
200 ml plain normal fat natural yoghurt
  or soy yoghurt
1 tbsp vegetable oil
2 tbsp butter
1 tsp sugar
1 tsp salt
1 cinnamon stick
4 cardamom pods
4 whole cloves
50 ml sultan raisins (yellow raisins)
1 tbsp grated fresh ginger
1 fresh green chilli pepper

FOR SERVING

basmati rice

[1] Cut fish fillets into bite-sized pieces. Pour yoghurt over fish pieces and let marinate for about an hour.

[2] Heat the oil and butter in a frying pan. Add cinnamon stick, crushed cardamom seeds, cloves and raisins. Sauté spices for a couple of minutes.

[3] Remove fish pieces one by one from the yoghurt and add to pan, making sure that they do not fall apart. Pour the rest of the yoghurt into the pan and add the salt and sugar. Let simmer for about 10 min. or until the fish is cooked through. Do not stir the sauce, to prevent the fish from disintegrating.

[4] Finally, split the chilli pepper and remove seeds. Add the chilli pepper and ginger to the sauce and serve hot with rice.

Fried Jumbo Prawns

500 g deveined jumbo prawns with tail intact
1 long red chilli pepper
2 cloves garlic
1 tbsp olive oil
1 tbsp sesame oil
1 tbsp sugar
juice and grated zest of 2 limes
1 tbsp soy sauce
1 tsp Thai fish sauce

[1] Mince chilli pepper and garlic.

[2] Heat oil in pan then add sugar, chilli pepper and garlic. Add prawns and fry quickly, for about 30 seconds.

[3] Mix lime juice, lime zest, soy sauce and fish sauce together and pour over prawns. Simmer.

[4] Serve with toasted bread or enjoy alone.

Blue Mussels and Pepper Salsa

1 kg fresh live blue mussels
1 large onion
3 cloves garlic
1 tbsp vegetable oil
1 tsp sea salt
1 tsp ground black pepper
100 ml minced fresh coriander
5 dried small red chillies
300 ml white wine
200 ml water

PEPPER SALSA

2 ripe tomatoes
1 small onion
1 clove garlic
3 tbsp white wine vinegar
1 tbsp maple syrup
1 tsp harissa (p. 174)
juice of ½ lemon
1 red pepper
1 yellow pepper
4 tbsp mussel cooking water

[1] Prepare salsa: Scald tomatoes, peel and dice. Dice onion, garlic and peppers. Mix all ingredients together. Add 4 tbsp mussel cooking water left over from boiling.

[2] Wash and clean blue mussels. Chop onion and garlic. Mince coriander and chillies.

[3] Put mussels in a large pot and sprinkle onions, coriander and chillies on top. Pour wine and water on top. Cover pot.

[4] Bring liquid to a boil and gently shake the pot. Boil for about 5 minutes, until the mussels have opened. Use only mussels that have opened.

[5] Remove outer shell from mussel. Place salsa on top of mussel meat and arrange for serving.

This amount is good as an hors d'oeuvre. If you wish to serve these as an entree, double the recipe.

A SERVANT LIVING IN THE SOUTH-WEST WING WAS IN THE HABIT OF SHAKING THE TABLECLOTHS OUT OF THE DINING ROOM WINDOW AFTER THE GENTLEFOLK HAD EATEN. SHE WATCHED THE BIRDS THROUGH THE FOGGED-UP WINDOW AS THEY PICKED UP EVERY LAST CRUMB. WHAT GREAT JOY CAN COME FROM EVEN THE SMALLEST BREAD CRUMB!

Anttu's
Prawn Pan

500 g prawns

MARINADE
1 fresh red chilli pepper
1 tbsp grated ginger
zest of 1 lime
3 tbsp olive or sesame oil
2 tsp herb salt
2 tsp ground black pepper

[1] Split the chilli pepper and remove seeds. Mince the chilli pepper.
[2] Mix marinade ingredients together and pour over prawns. Let marinate for a while in the refrigerator.
[3] Heat frying pan and fry prawns quickly, mixing and turning constantly.
[4] Serve with toasted bread or salad.

Thai Fish Sticks

FISH MINCE

400 g cod fillet
2 tbsp Omar's Curry Paste (p. 177)
1 egg yolk
100 ml potato flour
1 tsp baking powder
1 tbsp raw sugar
100 ml boiled green lentils

BREADING

1 egg and 1 leftover egg white
200 ml bread crumbs

FOR FRYING

rapeseed oil for deep frying

SAUCE

1 container sour cream or plain soy
  yoghurt
juice and grated zest of 1 lime
2 tbsp fresh coriander, minced

FOR SERVING

wasabi mashed potatoes (p. 71)

[1] Prepare sauce: Mix together sour cream, lime juice, lime zest and coriander. Put sauce in refrigerator.

[2] Boil green lentils according to pack instructions.

[3] Mix all fish stick ingredients, for example in a food processor. Form mince into fish sticks.

[4] Bake: Beat eggs gently with fork, breaking yolks. Roll fish sticks in egg and the bread using bread crumbs.

[5] Use a high-sided pan. Heat oil, which should be about 2 cm deep so that fish sticks can be immersed in oil. Place fish sticks in hot oil carefully and fry for about 5 min. Remove fish sticks with slotted spoon to drain on a plate covered with kitchen paper.

[6] Serve with wasabi mashed potatoes and coriander sauce.

Salmon with
Tan Lines

800 g wild-caught salmon fillet

MARINADE

4 tbsp coarse sea salt
4 tbsp grated fresh ginger
1 tbsp brown sugar
3 tbsp sesame oil
3 tsp minced Habanero chilli

YOU WILL ALSO NEED
clingfilm

FOR SERVING
lime slices

[1] Prepare marinade: Mix together sea salt, grated ginger, brown sugar, sesame oil and chilli pepper.

[2] Cut salmon fillet into four long slices. Brush salmon fillets with marinade.

[3] Tightly wrap each salmon fillet separately in clingfilm.

[4] Let wrapped fillets marinade in the refrigerator overnight.

[5] Removed clingfilm from fillets and brush away excess marinade.

[6] Heat grilling pan. Fry salmon fillets for a moment, until they have grill lines on the outside, but remain pink on the inside.

[7] Slice salmon and serve with lime slices.

Baking

···

"ODOURS IN THE EVENING MIST
SPICES THAT YOU CAN'T RESIST"

- PHISH: SPICES LYRICS

···

106

A Daughter examined her Mother's spice shelf. All of the spices were sealed in clear glass bottles, each of which was decorated with a hand-written sticker. The Daughter recited: "Coriander - for joint aches, stomach ache and difficulty breathing. Aphrodisiac." Only one bottle was empty and its lid was sealed shut. The Daughter was about to reach for the bottle, but Mother forbade her. "What could be in it that I should not open it?" the Daughter asked. "It contains a spice that will certainly get any stew bubbling. And then that bubbling never ends", said Mother. "It will feed many mouths, but when you taste that soup, you will never be able to get enough. Finally a person always drowns in that soup." The Daughter was horrified. "What sort of spice could that be?" Mother smiled: "That spice has many fine names, behind which it hides. It's real names are jealousy, bitterness, acrimony, hate, grudge-holding." The Daughter cringed. "Then why do you keep a jar like that among your spices?" "So that I will know it if anyone were to try to offer me some of it."

Sweet Tango Cookies

200 ml cashews
100 ml walnuts
3 organic eggs
100 ml free-flowing honey
100 ml sugar
zest of 1 orange
½ fresh red chilli pepper
500 ml flour or rice flour
2 tsp baking powder

[1] Heat oven to 175°C.

[2] Roast cashews in a dry, hot pan.

[3] Crush walnuts and cashews finely. Remove seeds from chilli pepper and mince it.

[4] Gently beat egg to break yolk. Add honey, sugar, orange zest, chilli pepper and ground nuts. Mix thoroughly.

[5] Mix dry ingredients and sift in with other ingredients. Knead mixture into a dough.

[6] Form dough into two 30 cm long flat rolls on a baking paper-covered cooking sheet.

[7] Bake rolls on oven centre rack for about 25-30 min. Remove rolls from oven and turn off power. Let cool slightly.

[8] Using a sharp knife, cut roll into slanting slices. Place slices on their sides on the baking sheet.

[9] Return cookies to oven and cook with residual heat for about half an hour.

The cookies are best after a few days. Serve them with a sweet dessert wine. Dip and enjoy!

Ginger's Muffins

400 ml rice or wheat flour
150 ml raw sugar
3 tsp baking powder
1 tsp bicarbonate of soda
¼ tsp salt
60 g grated dark chocolate
50 ml fresh grated ginger
1 ground star anise
1 organic egg
300 ml rice milk or milk
2 tbsp butter or margarine, melted

[1] Mix dry ingredients together. Sprinkle chocolate in.
[2] Mix egg, milk, melted butter and grated ginger in another container. Beat for a moment.
[3] Combine flour mixture with egg/milk mixture.
[4] Divide batter into muffin tins. Bake on oven centre rack at 175 degrees for approx 15-20 min.

You can modify this batter as you please. For example, try using grated coriander, fennel, cardamom or caraway seeds in place of ginger.

Inka's Lime Pie

SHORTCRUST

250 g butter or margarine
300 ml sugar
2 organic eggs
500 ml wheat flour or gluten free
  flour mixture
2 tsp baking powder
2 tsp vanilla sugar (p. 52)

FOR BUTTERING TIN

2 tbsp butter or margarine
bread crumbs

FILLING

400 ml sugar
8 organic eggs
400 ml double cream or soy cream
200 ml lime juice
zest of 2 limes
100 ml lemon juice
2 tbsp grated fresh ginger

GARNISH

fresh berries or fruit

[1] Prepare dough: Cream butter and sugar together until light. Whip in egg. Mix dry ingredients together and sift into dough. Mix. Let dough rest for a moment in the refrigerator.

[2] Heat oven to 180°C.

[3] Press shortcrust pastry onto bottom and about 6 cm up the sides of a springform cake tin which has been greased and sprinkled with bread crumbs. Pre-bake crust in oven for 10 min.

[4] In the meantime, prepare the filling. Beat sugar and eggs into a stiff foam.

[5] Carefully mix in cream, lime and lemon juices, lime zest and ginger.

[6] Pour filling into pre-baked crust and continue baking for approx. 45 minutes, until the pie begins to solidify.

[7] After removing from oven, pie will still be soft in the middle, but will solidify if you allow it to cool for about an hour.

[8] Garnish with fresh berries and fruits.

James Brownies

200 ml hazelnuts
175 g butter or margarine
300 ml sugar
150 ml dark cocoa powder
1 fresh red chilli pepper
50 ml golden syrup
¼ tsp salt
3 organic eggs
200 ml wheat or rice flour

FOR GREASING CAKE TIN

2 tbsp butter or margarine
bread crumbs

Icing suggestions:

CHOCOLATE ICING

250 ml double cream or soy cream
200 g dark chocolate
1 tsp butter

SUGAR ICING

400 ml pink, strawberry-flavoured
  icing sugar
2 tbsp water

[1] Heat oven to 175°C.
[2] Roast nuts in the oven for about 10 minutes to cause skins to loosen. Roll nuts in a kitchen towel against a table to remove the skins.
[3] Grease a 30 x 40 cm cake tin and sprinkle with bread crumbs.
[4] Cream together sugar and soft butter.
[5] Remove seeds from chilli pepper and mince.
[6] Mix in cocoa, syrup, chilli pepper and salt.
[7] Beat in eggs one at a time.
[8] Sift flour into dough and add hazelnuts. Mix carefully.
[9] Pour batter into cake tin and bake for 10-12 min. Let cool before making icing.
[10] Prepare chocolate icing: Bring cream to a boil and then remove from heat. Grate chocolate. Mix grated chocolate and butter with hot cream. Pour icing over cooled cake and let harden for a moment.

Alternatively, prepare pink icing by mixing icing sugar and water together.

baking

Jean's Deep Fried Nut Cookies

200 ml cashews
100 ml peeled pistachios
250 ml rice flour
1½ tsp caraway seeds
1 tbsp sesame seeds
1 tsp sea salt
1 tbsp grated fresh ginger
1 fresh green chilli pepper
20 g butter or margarine
2 organic eggs
3 tbsp water

FOR DEEP FRYING

300 ml rapeseed oil

¹ Remove seeds from chilli pepper.
² Grind nuts well in a liquidiser. Add chilli pepper, ginger, salt and butter to liquidiser. Mix.
³ Pour mixture into bowl and add eggs and water.
⁴ Mix until dough becomes sticky.
⁵ Heat oil for deep frying in a high-sided yet rather small saucepan.
⁶ Roll dough balls with a tablespoon and then pat to flatten slightly.
⁷ Deep fry for about 5 minutes, turning once during frying.
⁸ Drain excess oil from nut cookies on kitchen paper.

Polenta Bread [PICTURED]

200 ml rice or wheat flour
200 ml polenta
1 tsp sea salt
4 tsp baking powder
1 tbsp raw sugar
2 organic eggs
1 tbsp olive oil
300 ml milk or rice milk
1 green jalapeño chilli
1 red jalapeño chilli
1 tsp ground caraway seeds
1 tsp grated ginger
100 ml grated cheddar cheese

FOR GREASING BAKING TIN

vegetable oil

¹ Mix dry ingredients together.
² Mix in eggs, oil and milk. Mince jalapeños and add the remaining ingredients.
³ Grease non-stick bread tin.
⁴ Pour dough into tin and bake for 25 min at 190°C.

If you wish, you can substitute fresh herbs for the jalapeño, giving the bread a lovely herb scent.

Chocolate Chilli Bread [PICTURED]

700 ml wheat flour or gluten free
   flour mixture
½ tsp salt
2 tbsp butter or margarine
2 tbsp raw sugar
1 sachet dried yeast
2 tbsp dark cocoa powder
300 ml water
75 g dark chilli-flavoured chocolate
   (for example Plamil)

FOR GREASING

melted butter or margarine

[1] Heat oven to 220°C.
[2] Mix flour, salt, cocoa and dry yeast in a bowl.
[3] Add melted butter and lukewarm water.
[4] Knead dough by hand on a floured surface for about 10 min.
[5] Chop up chocolate and knead it into the dough.
[6] Divide dough in two and form into two bread loaves. Let loaves rise under a tea towel for just under an hour.
[7] Bake oven at 220°C for 10 min, then reduce heat to 190°C and bake for another 15-20 minutes.
[8] Oil loaves with melted butter and let cool covered.
[9] Serve with mascarpone or gorgonzola cheese.

Sweet Chilli Bread

500 ml rice or wheat flour
1½ tsp sea salt
2 (about 11 g total) sachets dried yeast
450 ml warm water
6 tbsp olive oil
2 cloves garlic
3 tbsp grated fresh ginger
4 tbsp fresh coriander
6 tbsp sweet chilli sauce

FOR GREASING BAKING TIN

2 tbsp butter or margarine
bread crumbs

[1] Mix dry ingredients together, including yeast.
[2] Add lukewarm water.
[3] Crush garlic cloves and grate ginger into mixture. Add chilli sauce.
[4] Mince fresh coriander and mix into dough.
[5] Grease bread tin and sprinkle with bread crumbs.
[6] Pour dough into tin and bake for 25-30 min at 200°C.
[7] Serve with salad.

Silk Road
Saffron Rolls

½ l milk or soy milk
50 g fresh yeast
2 tsp salt
500 ml whole meal flour or coarse
 gluten free flour mixture
500 ml flour or rice flour
300 ml grated carrot
a pinch of saffron
2 tbsp olive oil

GLAZE
200–300 ml warm water
1 tbsp honey

You can also use boiled carrots, which
should be blended with milk before
adding to the dough. You will need
4–5 carrots for this recipe.

[1] Heat milk until warm. Grate carrots.
[2] Pour milk into a container large enough for
the dough to rise. Crumble in yeast.
[3] Add salt, saffron and grated carrots to
dough.
[4] Gradually add flour, stirring dough all the
while.
[5] Leave dough to rise in a warm spot, covered
with a tea cloth.
[6] Form risen dough into rolls and let rise again
on baking sheet covered with baking paper.
[7] Brush rolls with honey water before baking,
which will give a beautiful colour and crisp
honey crust.
[8] Bake in oven at 225°C for 10-15 min.

Ramses II
Oat Cakes

200 g butter or margarine
200 ml sugar
150 ml honey
1 generous litre oatmeal
100 ml shredded coconut
50 ml pickled ginger
50 ml sunflower seeds or
    almond slivers

FOR GREASING BAKING TIN
vegetable oil or butter

[1] Melt butter in saucepan and add raw sugar and honey, stirring carefully.
[2] Chop pickled ginger.
[3] Add oatmeal and other ingredients to saucepan. Mix well.
[4] Spread oatmeal mixture in greased baking tin into a layer a few centimetres thick. You can pat the surface flat with wet hands. Bake at 180°C for 20 minutes.
[5] Let cool. Cut into square snacks.

Chilli Grissini

[PICTURED ON P. 150]

Makes about 25

15 g fresh yeast
1 tsp salt
1 tsp sugar
100 ml water
200 ml flour or rice flour
1 fresh red chilli pepper
2 tbsp olive oil

FOR GREASING
50 ml melted butter or margarine

[1] Heat oven to 200°C.
[2] Remove seeds from chilli pepper and mince. Mix sugar, salt, minced chilli pepper and yeast in warm water.
[3] Add flour a little at a time, mixing constantly, until the dough is elastic and no longer sticks to the sides of the bowl.
[4] Add olive oil. Knead dough for a moment more and then form it into a round loaf. Cover it with a cloth and let rest for about 10 minutes.
[5] Divide dough into 25 pieces and roll into thin, long sticks about half a centimetre thick. Place sticks on baking paper on baking sheet. Cover with a cloth and let rest for another 10 min.
[6] Brush sticks with melted butter and bake at 200°C for 10-15 minutes, until the sticks are a nice golden brown.

Desserts

· ·

"SEASONS CAME AND CHANGED THE TIME WHEN I GREW UP I CALLED HIM MINE HE WOULD ALWAYS LAUGH AND SAY REMEMBER WHEN WE USED TO PLAY"

– NANCY SINATRA: BANG BANG (MY BABY SHOT ME DOWN)

· ·

In one fleeting moment, the Wanderer met his Dream Goddess along the way, in whose form were combined all the virtues the Wanderer had longed for in his journeyings. The Goddess's arms and heart opened to the Wanderer, but the Wanderer hesitated. What would he now dream of, what would he now long for? The Goddess's eyes filled with tears and her mind with reluctant understanding as her eyes followed the Wanderer's back receding towards the horizon. The Wanderer knew his fate and was faithful to it.

Chocolate
Chilli Truffles

Makes about 24

100 ml crème fraîche or soft tofu
200 g dark chocolate
½ fresh red chilli pepper

GARNISH
dark cocoa powder or hundreds-and-thousands or shredded coconut

[1] Grate or chop chocolate. Heat crème fraîche or tofu and mix in chocolate. Mix until chocolate has melted.
[2] Remove seeds from chilli pepper and mince. Mix into chocolate mixture.
[3] Allow paste to cool first at room temperature and then for a few hours in the refrigerator.
[4] Form chocolate into truffle balls and then roll them in cocoa powder, hundreds-and-thousands or shredded coconut. You can also push nuts inside them.
[5] Store cold.

desserts

Auntie Anna's Ginger Compote

100 ml sugar
800 ml water
1 vanilla bean pod
7 dried apricots
1 tbsp grated fresh ginger

THICKENER

1-2 tbsp cold water
1 tbsp potato flour or cornflour

[1] Place apricots in 800 ml of water to soak two hours earlier.
[2] Heat saucepan and scorch sugar slightly. Stir constantly with wooden spatula to prevent the sugar from burning.
[3] Grate ginger.
[4] Add apricots, soaking water, vanilla pod and grated ginger to saucepan.
[5] Let simmer for about fifteen minutes.
[6] Purée with hand blender.
[7] Mix potato flour with a small amount of cold water and thicken soup. Bring to a boil and then remove from heat and allow to cool for a moment.
[8] Serve with whipped cream, for example.

Ginger Whipped Cream

MADE WITH SOY CREAM

1 carton soy double cream
1 tbsp maple syrup
2 tsp vanilla sugar (p. 52)
2 tsp pickled ginger, minced

[1] Prepare soy whipped cream according to package directions.
[2] Mix in minced pickled ginger.
[3] Serve on Ginger's Muffins (p. 110) or with berries.

DAIRY DOUBLE CREAM

1 carton double cream
1 tbsp maple syrup
2 tsp vanilla sugar (p. 52)
1 tsp lemon zest
2 tsp pickled ginger, minced

[1] Whip cream.
[2] Mix other ingredients into whipped cream.

"IN A DREAM THE STRANGEST AND THE ODDEST THINGS APPEAR AND WHAT INSANE AND SILLY THINGS WE DO. HERE IS WHAT I SEE BEFORE ME, VIVIDLY AND CLEAR: AS I RECALL IT, YOU WERE IN IT, TOO." – FRANK SINATRA: I HAD THE CRAZIEST DREAM

Fabulous
Fruit Salad

3 ripe peaches
3 ripe fresh figs or 7 dried figs
200 ml blueberries
500 ml strawberries

SYRUP DRESSING
300 ml water
1½ l sugar
juice and grated zest of 1 lemon
3 star anise
6 whole black peppercorns
5 whole cardamom seed pods
1 vanilla bean pod

[1] First prepare syrup. Heat water, sugar and lemon zest in saucepan, along with other spices except for lemon juice. Mix well and ensure that the sugar has dissolved before it reaches a boil.
[2] Simmer syrup for about 10 minutes on low heat.
[3] Remove syrup saucepan from heat and add lemon juice. Stir. Let cool. Do not remove whole spices yet, because the longer you leave them in, the more full the flavour will be.
[4] Prepare fruit and berry salad. Slice figs and peaches, cube strawberries and then sprinkle blueberries on top. Pour syrup over salad through sieve.

Sorbet Verde

2 ripe bananas
3 kiwis
100 g piece of fresh ginger
300 ml sugar
350 ml water
juice of 1 lemon

[1] Chop ginger finely. Boil water and sugar in saucepan. Stir in ginger. Let boil until sugar has dissolved. Remove saucepan from heat and let cool.

[2] Strain ginger out of sugar solution. Put sugar solution in refrigerator to cool.

[3] Purée bananas and kiwis and mix them with the cold sugar solution. Add lemon juice to mixture.

[4] Churn mass in ice cream machine and freeze. You can also freeze the sorbet without an ice cream machine, but remember to stir the mass a few times during freezing in order to achieve the proper consistency.

Cayenne Chocolate Dip

300 g dark chocolate
1 tsp cayenne pepper
or use dark chilli-flavoured chocolate,
 with at least 70% cocoa content,
 (for example Plamil)
2 tbsp honey

FOR DIPPING

macadamia nuts
Brazil nuts
cashews
fresh strawberries
cape gooseberries (physalis)

[1] Turn back cape gooseberry husks. Also leave strawberry caps so they are easier to hold while dipping.
[2] Melt chocolate in double boiler. Stir carefully with a wooden spatula, making sure that steam does not get into the chocolate.
[3] Mix cayenne pepper and honey into chocolate.
[4] Dip berries and nuts in chocolate sauce and set aside to cool on baking paper on a flat surface.
[5] Serve immediately.

Orange Valley Dessert Sauce

grated zest and juice of 2 oranges
1 tbsp brown sugar
1 tbsp sweet chilli sauce
2 tsp cornflour
2 tbsp water

[1] Grate orange zest with a fine grater straight into saucepan and then squeeze in orange juice.
[2] Add brown sugar and chilli sauce to saucepan. Bring to a boil.
[3] Mix cornflour with water in a separate cup and pour into sauce. Bring to a boil and simmer for about 2 minutes.
[4] Serve with vanilla ice cream, for example.

Cuban Strawberries

2 litres fresh strawberries
1 fresh red chilli pepper
100 ml dark rum
2 tbsp brown sugar
50 ml water

[1] Remove seeds from chilli pepper and mince.
[2] Pour water into small saucepan and bring to a boil. Mix in brown sugar, minced chilli and rum. Heat on medium heat until sugar has dissolved.
[3] Pour sauce over strawberries and serve with genuine vanilla ice cream.

Spicy Strawberries

fresh strawberries
cardamom/black pepper

[1] Grind cardamom or black pepper finely in a mortar.
[2] Halve strawberries and sprinkle cardamom or black pepper grinds over them.
[3] Serve with vanilla ice cream, for example.

White Chocolate Vanilla Mousse

2 large or 4 small servings

200 ml double cream or soy cream
 (p. 126)
150 ml whole milk or soy milk
1 vanilla bean pod
1 leaf gelatin
200 g white chocolate

[1] Place gelatin leaf in cold water to soak.

[2] Whip cream.

[3] Pour milk into saucepan. Split vanilla pod lengthwise and scrape seeds in with milk. Also add vanilla pod. Bring milk to a boil, but don't let it burn to the pan.

[4] Remove vanilla pod from milk. Mix gelatin leaf into milk after squeezing dry.

[5] Chop white chocolate into pieces and add to hot milk. Mix until chocolate has melted.

[6] When chocolate and milk mixture has cooled, mix in whipped cream.

[7] Spoon mousse into serving dishes and move to the refrigerator for a few hours before serving.

Mint Chocolate Milkshake [PICTURED]

½ l vanilla ice cream or vanilla soy
 ice cream
200 ml milk or soy milk
60 g grated dark chocolate
a handful of fresh mint

[1] Chop vanilla ice cream into pieces.

[2] Mix all ingredients in liquidiser and serve immediately.

Tapas

"AND DO I LOVE YOU MY OH MY
YEH RIVER DEEP MOUNTAIN HIGH
IF I LOST YOU WOULD I CRY"

- TINA TURNER: RIVER DEEP
- MOUNTAIN HIGH

The Expert was a Success Story at everything he attempted. The Analysts and Cynics scrambled to speculate about the Expert's strategies and calculations. They never discovered what the Expert's secret was. Not that the Expert was shouting it to anyone anyway. They would have thought he was joking, or raving mad, if he would have told the truth. The Expert's guiding principle was very simple. He read himself a fairytale every evening. In these tales, everything was possible and there was always a new path behind even the largest dragon. The Expert remembered something that the Analysts and Cynics had forgotten. If you retain the eyes of a child, then you see all of the doors of possibility as open to you.

Golden Carrots
and Courgettes

8 large carrots
1 medium courgette
2 tbsp vegetable oil
½ tsp saffron
2 tbsp sesame seeds
1 tsp ground black pepper
1 tsp sea salt
1 tbsp sesame oil

[1] Thinly slice carrots and courgettes lengthwise with a cheese slicer.
[2] Heat vegetable oil in a pan and add carrots. Sauté for a few minutes and add courgettes. Sauté for a few more minutes.
[3] Add spices (except sesame oil) and sesame seeds. Mix quickly.
[4] Arrange on serving dish and sprinkle sesame oil over vegetables. Serve hot or cold with crispy bread.

Chilli Almonds

200 ml almonds
20 g butter or margarine
2 tsp fine sea salt
1 tsp chilli powder

[1] Soak almonds in hot water for five minutes. Remove almond skins and dry using kitchen paper.
[2] Melt butter in frying pan and roast almonds until golden in hot butter.
[3] Dump almonds into a dish lined with kitchen paper and dab most of the butter off.
[4] Move almonds to another container. Mix sea salt and chilli powder with almonds, stirring quickly.

Spiced Mayonnaises

If you wish, you can substitute normal mayonnaise with egg-free or milk-free mayonnaise. They generally already contain sea salt, so check the flavour before adding salt.

CHILLI-PEPPER MAYONNAISE

200 ml mayonnaise
3 crushed cloves garlic
½ yellow pepper, cubed
1 fresh green chilli pepper
1 tsp sea salt
1 tsp ground black pepper

Mix all ingredients together.

GREEN AND PINK PEPPER MAYONNAISE

200 ml mayonnaise
1 tsp green peppercorns
1 tsp pink peppercorns
1 tsp sea salt

Crush peppercorns in mortar and mix all ingredients together.

REMOULADE – GYPSY KING SAUCE FOR ROADRUNNERS

100 ml minced celery stalks
100 ml minced spring onions
100 ml chopped parsley
2 tbsp Dijon mustard
3 crushed cloves garlic
2 tbsp grated horseradish or horseradish paste
½ tsp sea salt
200 ml mayonnaise

Mix all ingredients together.

AIOLI

200 ml mayonnaise
4 cloves garlic
1 tsp chilli powder

Mix all ingredients together.

Sweet-and-Sour Sauce

2 tbsp sugar
100 ml white wine vinegar or apple
  vinegar
1 fresh red chilli pepper
3 tbsp ketchup (p. 176) or tomato
  pureé
100 ml lukewarm water
1 tsp cornflour

[1] Remove seeds from chilli pepper and mince.
[2] Scorch sugar in saucepan for a moment and carefully add vinegar. Simmer on medium heat for about 5 min., until vinegar evaporates.
[3] Add other ingredients except cornflour. Simmer for a few minutes.
[4] Finally thicken with cornflour.

Forget learning Chinese. Instead use your time preparing sweet-and-sour sauce, enjoying food and perfecting your tai chi forms.

Yoghurt Dips

MANGO DIP

200 ml plain yoghurt
1 tin (approx. 400 g) canned mango
1 fresh red chilli pepper

Mince chilli pepper. Mix all ingredients together in a liquidiser.

LIME DIP

200 ml plain yoghurt
juice and grated zest of 1 lime
1 tsp cayenne pepper

Mix all ingredients together.

SWEET CHILLI DIP

200 ml plain yoghurt
1 tbsp sweet chilli sauce
1 tbsp free-flowing honey
juice and grated zest of ½ lemon

Mix all ingredients together.

Rhythmic Salsa

1 tsp finely minced Habanero chilli
300 g canned tomatoes
200 g canned roasted peppers
    (preserved in liquid in a glass jar)
6 spring onions
juice and grated zest of 1 lime
50 ml chopped fresh coriander
1 tsp sea salt
1 tsp ground black pepper

[1] Grate lime zest and squeeze juice.
[2] Mix all ingredients in a liquidiser or with a hand blender into a smooth paste.
[3] Serve at room temperature with grilled meat or as a dip with tortilla chips.

Jalapeño Salsa [PICTURED]

7 ripe tomatoes
4 whole canned jalapeños
1 tsp raw sugar
1 tsp sea salt
1 red onion
a bunch of fresh mint

[1] Remove heads from tomatoes. Chop tomatoes and jalapeños.
[2] Mince onions.
[3] Mix all ingredients and set aside in a cool spot.

AT THE END OF A JOURNEY THAT SEEMED TO LAST FOREVER, THE WANDERER ACHIEVED NIR-VANA: THE TOUCH OF THE JUICE OF THE FRESH MANGO BETWEEN HIS LIPS. THE WANDERER KNEW HE HAD REACHED THE GREATEST ISLAND OF HAPPINESS.

Caribbean Mojo

1 fresh mango
a slice of fresh pineapple 1 cm thick

1 avocado
juice of 2 limes
100 ml orange juice
2 tbsp fresh coriander, chopped
1 tsp raw sugar
2 tsp minced Habanero chilli
4 spring onions
1 tsp sea salt
1 tsp ground black pepper

[1] Chop mango, pineapple and avocado into 1 x 1 cm. cubes. Finely mince spring onion.
[2] Remove seeds from chilli pepper and mince.
[3] Mix all ingredients together. Cover container and place in refrigerator for half an hour before serving.
[4] Serve with baked fresh tuna fish.

Avocado Guacamole [PICTURED]

Chilli Grissini recipe p. 121, also pictured

2 avocados
juice of 1 lime
½ onion
2 cloves garlic
1 tsp cayenne pepper
½ tsp herb salt

GARNISH

½ red pepper

[1] Mix all ingredients with a liquidiser or hand blender.
[2] Dice pepper and use as garnish.

Easy Tomato Onion Mixture

4 ripe tomatoes
1 small fresh yellow chilli pepper
2 red onions
juice and grated zest of 1 lemon
1 tsp granulated sea salt
1 tsp ground black pepper

[1] Dice tomatoes. Mince garlic and chilli pepper.
[2] Grate lime zest and squeeze juice.
[3] Combine all ingredients and flavour with salt and pepper to taste.
[4] Serve cold.

Cleopatra's Aubergine Caviar

2 medium-size aubergines
juice and grated zest of 1 lemon
3 cloves garlic
1 fresh red chilli pepper
2 tbsp olive oil
1 tsp fine sea salt
2 tsp ground black pepper

[1] Grill aubergines whole in a grill or in casserole dish under oven grilling element set at 200°C for about 20 minutes. Turn frequently and cook until the skin blackens and the insides soften. While cooking, the aubergine will give off hot steam, so beware of burning your fingers!
[2] Set aubergines aside to cool. Peel once cooled and remove heads.
[3] Pureé peeled aubergines and other ingredients in a liquidiser or with a hand blender.
[4] Serve with bread or grilled Halloumi cheese.
[5] If you wish to use this paste as a dipping sauce, add olive oil and plain yoghurt or soy yoghurt.

Potato Crisps
à la Home

about 40-50 crisps

2-3 large potatoes

1 tsp paprika powder
½ tsp coriander powder
½ tsp caraway seeds
2 tsp sesame seeds
½ tsp cayenne pepper
olive oil or melted butter

[1] Heat oven to 170°C.
[2] Mix spices and sesame seeds together.
[3] Peel potatoes and slice very thin.
[4] Place potato slices on baking paper and sprinkle with olive oil. Sprinkle spice mixture carefully over slices.
[5] Bake in oven for about 30-40 minutes, until the slices become crisp and have some colour. Place crisps on kitchen paper so the most part of the fat can drip off. Cool and serve with dip (p. 145).

Sticky Paws
Spicy Nuts

[PICTURED]

400 ml nuts, such as cashews and
  walnuts
100 ml free-flowing honey
1 tsp cinnamon powder
1 tsp powdered ginger
½ tsp cardamom powder
½ tsp chilli powder

[1] Heat oven to 200°C.
[2] Mix spices with honey and add nuts.
[3] Pour nuts into oven-proof dish and roast in hot oven for about 10 min. Use a spoon to form small globs on a plate or in small muffin cases. Let cool. Put nut balls in refrigerator to solidify before serving.

Drinks

∙∙

"YOU'RE THE CREAM IN MY COFFEE
YOU'RE THE SALT IN MY STEW YOU
WILL ALWAYS BE MY NECESSITY I'D
BE LOST WITHOUT YOU"

- NAT KING COLE: YOU'RE THE
CREAM IN MY COFFEE"

∙∙

Hemmed in by numerous standing ovations, the Opera Diva felt herself alone, but thankfully champagne had been invented. Gentlemen showered her with beautiful diamonds and other bangles, but none of the Gentlemen was able to reach the Diva's heart. The resplendence of the society into which she was invited was almost blinding and the shouts of hurrah almost deafening, and the Diva no longer saw or heard how many zeros there were after the Gentlemen's expressions of affection. It was all the same; they were all empty zeros. Until a change occurred. The Diva's voice failed. What to do with a Diva without a voice? For some time things went on as before, a champagne glass in her hand as she was paraded through the cocktail parties, but when the zeros and diamonds began to flow to new addresses, she suddenly came to the bottom of her glass. Then the Diva had an idea. Even though her voice didn't work, she still had some damn fine lungs. And that was when the Diva's glass blowing hobby began. She blew bottles, glasses, cups and bowls, each larger, grander and more resplendant than the last. But this time she paid close attention that the Gentlemen could not put her inside a glass bowl again!

Mint Refresher

[PICTURED]

700 g plain soy yoghurt
 or yoghurt
50 ml honey
zest of ½ lime
a handful of fresh mint
50 ml soy cream or dairy double
 cream

GARNISH
mint leaves

[1] Grate lime zest.
[2] Mix all ingredients together in liquidiser.
[3] Let rest for a moment in the refrigerator.
[4] Garnish with mint leaves and serve.

Coco's Mango Cocktail

4 glasses full

1 tin (approx 400 g) canned mango
 with sugar syrup
2 tbsp grated fresh ginger
200 ml mineral water

You can give these cocktails a bite with clear alcohol.

[1] Open mango tin. Put mangos and sugar syrup in the freezer for 3-4 hours in a freezer-safe container.
[2] Mix all ingredients together in a liquidiser. Serve in cocktail glasses.

"I'VE LEARNED THAT THE WAYS IN WHICH AN INDIVIDUAL HANDLES THE FOLLOWING THREE THINGS TELLS A LOT ABOUT HIM: A RAINY DAY, LOST LUGGAGE AND TANGLED CHRISTMAS DECORATIONS." - UNKNOWN

Vampire Vamp's Tomato Drink for a Big Hit

4 glasses full

1 tsp horseradish paste
½ tsp ground black pepper
¼ tsp sea salt
1 tin (400 g) chopped tomatoes
2 drops of Tabasco
juice of 1 lime
1 tsp dried oregano
8 ice cubes

GARNISH
lime slices
lemon balm leaves

[1] Mix all ingredients together in a liquidiser. Add ice gradually to allow the machine to operate properly.
[2] Serve in transparent glasses and garnish with lemon balm and limes.
[3] If you wish, this recipe makes a marvellous Bloody Mary base. Appropriate liquors for this drink include Tequila and vodka.

Marianne Moon Cocktail [PICTURED]

4 glasses full

500 ml firm strawberries
200 ml red juice
50 ml ground-up mint chocolate sweets

GARNISH
ground black pepper
a few mint leaves

You can give this cocktail a kick by adding vanilla-flavoured vodka.

[1] Mix all ingredients together in a liquidiser.
[2] Pour drink in glasses.
[3] Grind some black pepper on top and garnish with mint leaves.

Basil-Chilli Martini

4 glasses full

160 ml Martini Bianco
a handful of basil leaves
a piece of fresh red chilli pepper
   2 cm long
crushed ice

[1] Crush basil leaves and minced chilli pepper
into base of shaker.
[2] Add crushed ice and martini. Shake
vigorously. Strain drink into cocktail glasses.

Mary's Mint Drink

4 glasses full

600 ml pear juice
200 ml mineral water
200 ml canned pears, chopped
crushed ice
a handful of mint leaves

GARNISH
Edible flowers or pink sweets

You can give this drink a kick by
adding Vodka.

[1] Mix all ingredients in liquidiser and pour
into decorative glasses.
[2] Garnish with edible flowers or pink sweets.

drinks

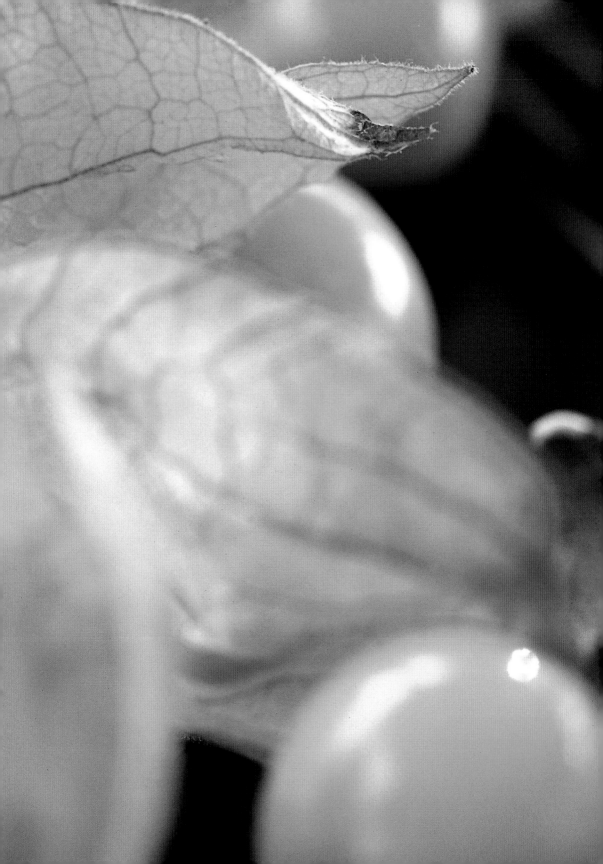

Cool Cinnamon Tea

1 l brewed cinnamon tea, for example
   Yogi Classic
5 star anise
2 cinnamon sticks
a bundle of cinnamon basil with stems
   or regular basil
ice cubes

[1] Prepare tea and cool.
[2] Pour tea into a jug and add spices.
[3] If desired, sweeten with honey.
[4] Store in refrigerator and serve with ice
cubes.

Cool Tea

1 l cold water
2 bags black tea or 1 tbsp
   tea leaves
1 bag black tea or 1 tbsp
   tea leaves
juice and shredded zest of one orange
1 tbsp sugar or honey
2 tsp vanilla sugar (p. 52)
1 vanilla bean pod
ice cubes

YOU WILL ALSO NEED

a large plastic bottle or jug in which
you can store the drink in the
refrigerator.

[1] Wash the orange carefully in warm water
and then take peelings from zest using a
peeler before you squeeze the juice.
[2] Mix all ingredients together and let soak for a
few minutes at room temperature. Later place
the jug in the refrigerator. The best results are
had by leaving letting the drink soak overnight.
[3] Remove tea bags before serving.
[4] Vanilla pod can be reused.

English Cooling Spiced Tea

1 l lukewarm water
4 cloves
1 cinnamon stick
3 bags Earl Grey
juice of 1 lemon
2 tbsp sugar or honey
a bunch of fresh lemon balm leaves

Add all ingredients to jug of warm water and
let soak. After tea has cooled, place jug in
refrigerator. The drink will be ready after a
few hours. If you wish, you may also boil this
spiced tea and then enjoy hot.

Café de olla Cinnamon Coffee [PICTURED]

4 coffee cups of water
50 ml dark sugar, for example
  Muscovado
1 cinnamon stick
4 whole cloves
4 tbsp dark roast coffee grinds

[1] Heat all ingredients besides coffee in a saucepan. Stir until sugar has dissolved.
[2] Add coffee grinds and bring to a boil. Let brew covered for 5 minutes.
[3] Mix before serving and strain into coffee mugs.

Chilli Cocoa

50 g dark chilli-flavoured chocolate
  (over 70% cocoa content, for
  example Plamil)
500 ml milk or soy milk
2 tbsp sugar
1 tsp ground cloves
½ tsp cinnamon powder

FOR SERVING
ginger whipped cream (p 126)

[1] Grate or chop chocolate. Heat milk and mix in chopped-up chocolate.
[2] Add the rest of the ingredients and whip.
[3] Serve with whipped cream.

Cinnamon Cocoa

50 g dark chocolate
450 ml milk or soy milk
1 tsp vanilla sugar (p. 52)
½ tsp cinnamon powder
1 tbsp sugar

"SPOONS"
4 cinnamon sticks

[1] Grate or chop chocolate. Heat milk and mix in chopped-up chocolate.
[2] Add the rest of the ingredients and whip.
[3] Pour into serving dishes and place one cinnamon stick in each as a spoon.

Spice Mixtures

Curry Spice Mixture

6 small dried chilli peppers
8 tbsp coriander seeds
4 tbsp cumin seeds
2 tsp fenugreek seeds
2 tsp black mustard seeds
2 tsp whole black peppercorns
1 tbsp turmeric powder
1 tsp powdered ginger

[1] Remove seeds from chilli peppers.
[2] Roast chillies, coriander, cumin, fenugreek, mustard seeds and peppercorns in a hot, dry pan. Mix carefully with a wooden spatula, making sure the mixture doesn't burn. Let cool before grinding.
[3] Grind all ingredients into a fine powder in a spice mill or mortar and then finally add the turmeric and ginger powders.

Sri Lankan Curry

6 tbsp coriander seeds
3 tbsp cumin seeds
1 tbsp fennel seeds
1 tsp fenugreek seeds
1 tsp cinnamon powder
1 tsp whole cloves
8 cardamom pods
6 dried curry leaves
2 tsp chilli powder

[1] Roast coriander, cumin, fennel and fenugreek in a hot, dry pan. Mix well.
[2] Add cinnamon, cloves and cardamom pods and roast for a moment more, stirring carefully.
[3] Remove pods from cardamom seeds.
[4] Grind all ingredients into powder in a spice mill or mortar.

Gomasio
Sesame Salt

6 tbsp sesame seeds
1 tbsp sea salt

[1] Roast sesame seeds in a hot pan, stirring well, until the seeds start to "pop" and jump about. Be careful not to burn.
[2] Pour roasted seeds into mortar. Add salt. Crush thoroughly.

Sesame salt can be used in food preparation or sprinkled over complete dishes. Healthy and delicious!

Tandoori Masala
Spice Mixture

4 tsp coriander seeds
4 tsp cumin seeds
2 tsp turmeric powder
4 tsp garlic powder
2 tsp powdered ginger
2 tsp mango powder
4 tsp paprika powder
2 tsp chilli powder
2 tsp dried mint

[1] Roast coriander and cumin in a hot, dry pan, stirring well.
[2] Grind roasted ingredients into powder in a spice mill or mortar and add remaining ingredients.

Fantastic
Spice Mixture

4 tbsp basmati rice (dry, not cooked)
3 tbsp cumin seeds
4 tbsp coriander seeds
1 tbsp black mustard seeds
1 tbsp whole black peppercorns
1 tbsp fenugreek seeds
1 tsp whole cloves
4 tbsp turmeric powder

[1] Roast basmati rice in a hot, dry pan for about 3 minutes or until the rice has turned a beautiful golden colour. Set rice aside to cool.
[2] Roast other ingredients except for turmeric for about 3 minutes.
[3] Add spices to rice and let cool. Grind all ingredients into powder in a spice mill or mortar. Finally add turmeric powder. Store in an air-tight container.

This spice mixture will turn any dish into a delicacy fit for a king, the nutty flavour of the basmati rice perfectly complementing the aromas of the other spices.

Sweet English Spice Mixture

2 tsp ground pepper (black, white or
    pink pepper blend)
4 tsp cinnamon powder
2 tsp ground cloves
2 tsp ground nutmeg
2 tsp powdered ginger

Mix all ingredients.

SUGGESTED USES

–Dry cakes
–Puddings
–Crème brûlée
–Ice cream

Spice Mixture for Baking

1 tsp ground cloves
1 tsp powdered cinnamon
1 tsp ground nutmeg

Mix all ingredients together.

SUGGESTED USES

– Dry cakes
– Apple pies
– Rhubarb pies

Dukkah – Cleopatra's Spice Mixture

200 ml peeled pistachios
200 ml almonds
1 tbsp coriander seeds
1 tbsp cumin seeds
1 tbsp dried thyme
50 ml sesame seeds
½ tsp sea salt

[1] Roast pistachios and almonds in a hot, dry
pan, until they change colour. Stir carefully.
[2] Set the nuts aside to cool.
[3] Also roast coriander, cumin, thyme and
sesame seeds briefly. Stir carefully.
[4] Combine all ingredients and crush them in
a mortar. This spice mixture should end up
being a dry, crumbly mixture, not a paste.

SERVING SUGGESTIONS

- Dip fresh bread first in olive oil, then in the
dukkah. YUM!
- You can also top bread by sprinkling with
olive oil, crumbling some dukkah into the oil
and then toasting the bread in the oven. An
excellent side dish for soups!
- You can also use dukkah for breading in
place of bread crumbs.
- Also try with pastas to give them an exotic
flavour.

Harissa

1 tbsp sunflower oil
1 red pepper
3 long fresh red chillies
2 cloves garlic
1 tbsp coriander seeds
1 tbsp cumin seeds
2 tbsp tomato purée
1 tsp coarse sea salt
1 tsp crushed black pepper

[1] Remove seeds from chilli pepper and chop.
[2] Slice the garlic and chillies.
[3] Heat oil in a pan and add all ingredients. Sauté for about 10 minutes, until the pepper is quite soft.
[4] Mix all ingredients into a paste using a hand blender. You can add a little oil as needed.
[5] Store in an air-tight container in the refrigerator. Harissa will keep for about 2 weeks in the refrigerator.

Indian Marinade

300 ml plain yoghurt or
    soy yoghurt
1 tbsp curry spice mixture (p. 170)
1 tsp cayenne pepper
1 tsp ground cardamom
2 tbsp dried mint
½ tsp sea salt
1 tsp ground black pepper
1 clove garlic
juice of 1 lime
2 tbsp olive or sunflower oil

Crush garlic clove and mix all ingredients together. Let rest in the refrigerator for couple of hours.

This marinade works well for grilled vegetables. You can also turn it into a sauce for roast potatoes by increasing the amount of yoghurt.

Herbs de Provence Spice Mixture

3 tbsp dried thyme
2 tbsp dried mint
1 tsp dried rosemary
3 dried sage leaves
1 tsp dried lavender

Mix all ingredients and grind to a powder with a mortar, if you want a finer spice mixture.

Kingston Jerk
Spice Paste

Even Bob Marley would slip from his cloud
if he tasted this!

6 small dried chilli peppers
2 spring onions with stalks
3 cloves garlic
1 tsp grated fresh ginger
3 tbsp fresh thyme
1 tbsp ground mixed peppercorns
2 tsp ground black pepper
1 tsp cinnamon powder
1 tsp ground nutmeg
1 tsp ground cloves
50 ml sunflower oil

[1] Mix all ingredients in a liquidiser or with a hand blender into a smooth paste.
[2] Add a little water or oil as needed.
[3] Store in an air-tight container in the refrigerator.

Spicy
Ketchup

10 ripe tomatoes or 1 tin crushed
   tomatoes
1 red pepper
zest and fruit of 1 orange

1 red onion
1 tbsp olive oil
50 ml sugar
2 tbsp red wine vinegar
1 tsp cayenne pepper
1 tbsp tamari or some other soy sauce

[1] Grate orange zest and chop fruit.
[2] Remove seeds from pepper. Cube pepper and tomatoes.
[3] Slice red onion and sauté in olive oil.
[4] Mix all ingredients together into ketchup using a hand blender. If you wish, you can add olive oil to make the ketchup runnier.

Omar's Curry Paste

50 ml dried small red chilli peppers
1 tsp whole black peppercorns
2 tsp cumin seeds
5 cardamom seed pods
1 tsp cinnamon powder
1 tsp coriander seeds
2 tsp paprika powder
1 onion
2 cloves garlic
2 tsp grated fresh ginger
1 tbsp oil
1 tsp honey

[1] Place chillies in a bowl and pour enough boiling water over to cover them. Let soak for about 15 minutes.
[2] Roast spices, excepting the onion, garlic and ginger, for a moment in a hot, dry pan.
[3] Chop onion and garlic.
[4] Remove chillies from water and save a little of the soaking water for the final stage of the paste.
[5] Grind roasted ingredients into powder in a spice mill or mortar.
[6] Mix chillies, onions and powdered spices into a paste in a food processor or with a hand blender. Add a little of the chilli soaking water so the paste becomes soft.
[7] Pour paste into a hot pan, adding oil and honey. Stir for a moment. Cool paste and store in an air-tight container.

Green Curry Paste

1 tbsp coriander seeds
1 tsp cumin seeds
1 whole star anise
10 fresh, small green hot chillies
1 onion
3 cloves garlic
a piece of galangal root about 3 cm
   long or 2 tsp galangal paste
2 stems lemon grass or 3 tsp paste
8 kaffir lime leaves
1 tsp whole black peppercorns
3 tbsp water

[1] Roast coriander, cumin and anise seeds in a hot, dry pan for a few minutes.
[2] At the same time, peel lemon grass and only use the centre part.
[3] Grind roasted ingredients into powder in a spice mill or mortar.
[4] Blend chopped chillies, onion, garlic, galangal, sliced lemon grass, lime leaves and pepper with a hand blender. Mix all ingredients into a paste and add a little water as needed.
[5] Store paste in an air-tight container. It will keep for about 2-3 weeks.

Yellow Curry Paste

1 tbsp coriander seeds
1 tsp cumin seeds
2 tsp turmeric powder
3 long fresh yellow chillies
1 onion
3 cloves garlic
2 stems lemon grass or 3 tsp paste
1 tsp whole pink peppercorns
3 tbsp sunflower oil

[1] Roast coriander and cumin seeds in a hot, dry pan for a few minutes.
[2] At the same time, peel lemon grass and only use the centre part.
[3] Grind roasted ingredients into powder in a spice mill or mortar.
[4] Blend chillies, onion, garlic, turmeric, sliced lemon grass and pink pepper with a hand blender. Mix all ingredients into a paste and finally add the oil.
[5] Store paste in an air-tight container. It will keep for about 2-3 weeks.

INDEX

CONTENTS

THANKS

Dish and textile loans

Formwerk
Kiinasoppi
Mateus-astiat/Temp
Kellopeli
Alexandran kammari
Moko
Ikea Espoo
Indiska Iso Omena
K-Rauta Suomenoja
Miun

To Pia, because your photos are heavenly.
To everyone whom we have loved, do love and
will yet come to love.
The band, Humane, for lyrics that caress the
soul and melodies that make us move.

184